# Amazing Earth

Written by Anita Ganeri

Illustrated by Tim Smart

With a foreword by
Steve Backshall

**Author** Anita Ganeri
**Illustrator** Tim Smart
**Subject Consultant** Dr Jonathan Dale

**Senior Editors** Dawn Sirett and James Mitchem
**Project Art Editor** Charlotte Bull
**Project Designer** Samantha Richiardi
**Project Editor** Francesco Piscitelli
**Additional Editing** Robin Moul
**Jacket Designer** Charlotte Bull
**Jacket Illustrator** Neil Den
**Jacket Coordinator** Issy Walsh
**Picture Researcher** Rituraj Singh
**Managing Editor** Penny Smith
**Production Editor** Dragana Puvacic
**Production Controller** John Casey
**Deputy Art Director** Mabel Chan
**Publishing Director** Sarah Larter

First published in Great Britain in 2021
by Dorling Kindersley Limited
One Embassy Gardens, 8 Viaduct Gardens,
London, SW11 7BW

The authorised representative in the EEA is
Dorling Kindersley Verlag GmbH. Arnulfstr. 124,
80636 Munich, Germany

A CIP catalogue record for this book
is available from the British Library.
ISBN: 978-0-2414-5945-4

Printed and bound in China

For the curious
www.dk.com

This book was made with Forest Stewardship
Council ™ certified paper – one small step in
DK's commitment to a sustainable future.
For more information go to
www.dk.com/our-green-pledge

# CONTENTS

# FOREWORD

Green, pink, and white smoke billowing across an Arctic night sky, like a giant genie released from its bottle. A neon skyscraper toppling in slow motion from an enormous ice cliff, kicking up a wave across a bay, and causing icebergs to rock and buck in the swell. Sand dunes singing and humming in desert winds under a blazing sun, and at night, lying under skies so clear it seems you could reach out and grasp the stars with your fingertips. Waking at the top of a towering Bornean ironwood tree to the sounds of whooping gibbons echoing over the misty canopy. Mexican forests where clouds of butterflies are so thick, they can break the branches they rest upon. The sight of the sun rising over Everest and setting over Chad's Ennedi Plateau. Victoria Falls at the end of the rainy season. The Amazon rainforest. The Congo River. The Deep.

The real miracles of Planet Earth defy description.

Not so long ago, it was my privilege to be the first person for millennia to stand inside a limestone cavern where the walls are emblazoned with handprints and animal paintings that date back at least 40,000 years. The thing that struck our team more than anything was that, although everything has changed in our world since then, our sense of perspective is still the same. We found that the highest concentrations of cave art are at the places with the best view of the surrounding landscapes, or on pale walls that are turned into giant cinema screens by the full moon. Those people tens of thousands

of years ago essentially wanted the same things we do: security, sanctuary, full bellies, and a warm dry place to lay their heads… but they also saw beauty, just as we do now. And although it might perhaps be stretching the point, we were struck by another sight in the forests of Suriname, when we discovered an unknown waterfall: we found jaguar poo at the very finest viewpoint of the falls. It was impossible to avoid thinking that this magnificent cat had come there — like us — to enjoy the view!

The natural wonders in this book will have been intoxicating human beings and their relatives since the dawn of time. They have given rise to religions and beliefs, with Indigenous peoples across the planet revering the spirit in every rock and tree, and holding each high and dramatic place sacred.

Enjoy the timeless wonders in these pages, but perhaps when you're done, give some thought to the fact that they have survived extinction events and deep time, but many of these fabulous places are now facing their greatest challenge. Us.

Steve Backshall MBE
BAFTA and Emmy-winning wildlife
presenter, naturalist, and explorer

Steve

# WORLD MAP

Smoking Hills,
Canada

## North America

Silfra Rift,
Iceland

Giant's Causeway,
Northern Ireland

Grand Prismatic Spring,
USA

Fly Geyser, USA

Firefall, USA

Antelope Canyon,
USA

Singing Sand
Dunes,
USA

In North America,
be amazed by the
eye-catching colours
of Fly Geyser.

In Europe,
visit the stunning,
naturally formed rock
pillars of the legendary
Giant's Causeway.

Cenote Ik Kil,
Mexico

Great Blue Hole,
Caribbean Sea,
off the coast
of Belize

Mount Roraima, along
the border of Brazil,
Venezuela, and Guyana

## Amazing journey

From a freezing ice shelf off the coast
of Antarctica to a hot salt lake in Africa,
and from a towering mountain in South
America to a vast meteor crater in Australia,
this book is packed with stunning locations
from all seven continents of the world.

On your travels, you'll visit a range of
landscapes and habitats, with different
climates and features. For each place,
you'll find a small world map that
shows you where you are. Here,
you can see all the places together.
Where will you start your adventure?

Lençóis
Maranhenses,
Brazil

## South America

Salar de Uyuni,
Bolivia

Marble Caves
(Cuevas de Mármol),
on the border
of Chile and
Argentina

In South America,
take a boat trip to
the sparkling blue
Marble Caves.

Trolltunga,
Norway

North Frisian Islands,
Germany

Europe

Asia

Lake Baikal,
Russia

Valley of the
Geysers,
Russia

Pamukkale,
Turkey

The Dead Sea,
on the border
of Jordan
and Israel

Zhangjiajie
Mountains, China

Chinoike Jigoku,
Japan

Valley of the
Whales,
Egypt

Meghalaya
Root Bridges,
India

Ban Gioc Waterfall,
Vietnam

In Asia, take a
trek to the pointy
Zhangjiajie Mountains,
topped with forests.

Manjanggul
Cave,
South Korea

Africa

Ha Long Bay,
Vietnam

Lake Natron,
Tanzania

Socotra
Archipelago,
Yemen

Chocolate Hills,
Philippines

Ngorongoro
Crater,
Tanzania

Sea of Stars,
Maldives

Oceania

Skeleton Coast,
Namibia

Tsingy de
Bemaraha,
Madagascar

Wolfe Creek
Crater,
Australia

In Australia, travel to
Lake Hillier where the
water is bubble-gum pink.

Waitomo
Glowworm Caves,
New Zealand

Deadvlei and
Sossusvlei,
Namibia

Lake Hillier,
Australia

# If you're an avid explorer,
# turn the page...

In Africa, take an
eerie trip to the
Skeleton Coast.

Off the coast of Antarctica,
wonder at the Ross Ice Shelf,
which is bigger than
a country.

Ross Ice Shelf,
Ross Sea, off the
coast of Antarctica

Antarctica

Silfra Rift, Iceland

# SILFRA RIFT

At the stunningly beautiful Silfra Rift in Iceland, it's possible to explore a magical world between two moving plates of the Earth's crust. Here, divers can see more than a hundred metres ahead in the clear water and, in narrow parts of the rift, touch the continents of North America and Europe at the same time.

Divers use a platform at one end of the rift to exit the water. They enter via stairs that lead to another platform under the water.

# MOVING STORY

Running some 16,000 km (10,000 miles) down the middle of the Atlantic Ocean is a vast chain of mountains called the Mid-Atlantic Ridge. It separates two of Earth's tectonic plates — the North American Plate and the Eurasian Plate.

## Tectonic plates

The Earth's crust (its outermost surface) is cracked into giant slabs of rock called tectonic plates. They carry the land (continental crust) and the oceans (oceanic crust).

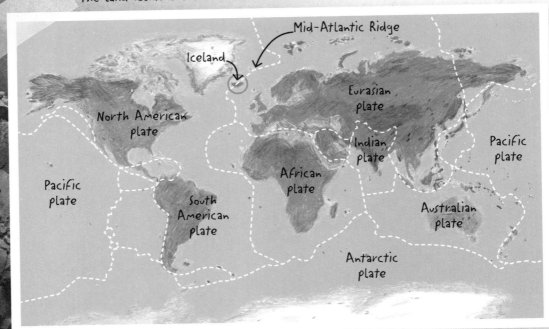

The tectonic plates are constantly moving — pulling apart, coming together, or sliding past each other.

At an ocean ridge, such as the Mid-Atlantic Ridge, the plates pull slowly apart. Magma rises to fill the gap, and forms new seabed, creating the ridge.

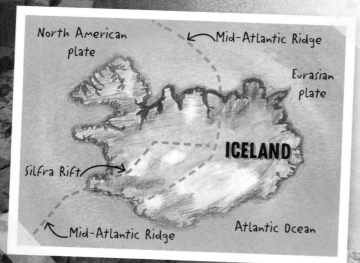

## The creation of rifts

Most of the Mid-Atlantic Ridge lies underwater, but parts of it rise above sea level, creating islands, such as Iceland. As the North American and Eurasian Plate move apart, stress builds up and causes earthquakes. These create cracks called rifts, such as the Silfra Rift, in the Earth's crust along the Mid-Atlantic Ridge.

## Scuba in Silfra

The Silfra Rift lies at the edge of Thingvallavatn Lake, in the Thingvellir National Park. It is about 300 m (985 ft) long and a maximum of 63 m (206 ft) deep. Divers can swim between solidified magma cliffs. The water is clear enough to see more than 100 m (328 ft) ahead. Divers are not allowed to go deeper than 18 m (60 ft) and must wear drysuits to keep warm.

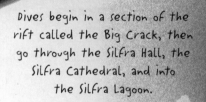

Dives begin in a section of the rift called the Big Crack, then go through the Silfra Hall, the Silfra Cathedral, and into the Silfra Lagoon.

The narrow Silfra Rift is at the edge of Thingvallavatn Lake.

Bright green "troll's hair" algae

## Clear waters

The water in the Silfra Rift comes from a glacier some 50 km (30 miles) long. Glacier meltwater is often murky, but here volcanic rock filters this water, leaving it crystal clear. Due to the fresh water constantly flowing in, the rift's water is cold, but never freezes. It stays at 2 to 4°C (36 to 39°F) all year round. There are fish in Thingvallavatn Lake, but few visit the rift. The rift does have plenty of plant life though — bright green "troll's hair" and other types of algae grow in large clumps on the rocks.

Chocolate Hills, Philippines

# CHOCOLATE HILLS

Fly over Bohol Island in the Philippines in the dry season, and you'll see an unusual landscape below — hundreds of small, round, brown hills spread out like a box of chocolates. Lush plants grow in the tropical monsoon climate, and there are rainforests and rice fields surrounding the grass-covered hills.

The island is home to the tiny Philippine tarsier, one of the world's smallest primates.

# CORAL CREATION

The Chocolate Hills are made from limestone rock covered in grass. Many scientists believe that they are the remains of ancient coral reefs (the limestone was created by the coral). Over time, rainfall has smoothed them into their current shape.

## How the hills may be the remains of coral reefs

Coral reef

Sea

Ground (seabed)

About 2 million years ago, this area lay under shallow sea. Coral reefs covered the seabed.

Limestone rock (made by the coral) cracked as it was pushed up.

Ground

Movement of the Earth's crust caused the land to rise out of the sea, exposing the coral reefs.

Rain eroded the exposed rock (more easily in the cracks).

Very slowly, rain eroded the limestone, eventually shaping it into round humps — the Chocolate Hills.

## Like chocolates in a box

There are more than a thousand hills, almost identical in shape. None are very high. The tallest is only 120 m (393 ft). In the rainy season, the hills are covered in green grass. In the dry season, the grass dies and turns brown, giving the hills their name.

Green grass covers the hills in the tropical rainy season.

In the dry season, the grass dies and turns the hills brown.

## Tarsier sanctuary

Apart from the Chocolate Hills, Bohol Island's main attraction is the Philippine Tarsier Sanctuary. This protected patch of rainforest is home to hundreds of these beautiful but endangered animals.

*Tarsiers hunt insects at night. They have huge, saucer-shaped eyes for seeing in the dark.*

## Legend says

Local legend tells of an imaginary story about how the hills were created by two rival giants. During a fight lasting several days, the giants hurled rocks and stones at each other. Finally, exhausted, they called a truce, and soon afterwards, left the island, abandoning their boulder-filled battlefield.

Trolltunga, Norway

# TROLLTUNGA

Some 700 m (2,300 ft) above a lake in Norway, a large slab of rock juts out into the air. This dramatic natural feature is called "Trolltunga" (Swedish for "troll's tongue") and is located in the southern Norwegian fjords. This area's mountain climate is cold, wet, and windy for most of the year.

There's a stunning view from the tip of the troll's tongue, but you'll need a head for heights.

# TROLL'S TONGUE

Trolltunga was formed during the last ice age, around 10,000 years ago. At that time, huge glaciers were slowly moving through this area of Norway. Meltwater from the glaciers flowed into cracks in the hard gneiss rock that is found here. The water then froze, causing the rock to break.

## How Trolltunga formed

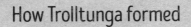

Broken rock    Glacier

Meltwater

Gneiss rock

Trolltunga

Gneiss rock

Meltwater from glaciers froze into cracks in the hard gneiss rock, causing chunks of the rock to break off and leaving some jagged rock edges behind.

As the glaciers moved away, they left behind the broken and jagged rocks, one of which was Trolltunga.

## Troll tales

There are many tales about trolls in Norway. These mythical beings are said to turn to stone in the sunlight, so they live in gloomy caves and only leave home after dark. In one such tale, a foolish troll doesn't believe that he is in any danger, and to prove it, he sticks his tongue out at the sun… allegedly forming Trolltunga.

TROLLTUNGA

It isn't likely to happen for thousands of years, but the boulder will eventually fall due to movement and cracks in the rocks.

The area is home to one of the largest herds of wild reindeer in Europe. They graze on grass and lichen.

## Balancing boulder

Another amazing rock formation in the southern Norwegian fjords is Kjeragbolten, a large boulder (deposited by a glacier long ago). It's wedged between two rocks, high up on Kjerag Mountain, and suspended 984 m (3,230 ft) above a deep, plunging drop.

## Hard hike

Trolltunga is a popular destination for hikers. The 27-km (17-mile) round trip, over steep, rocky, and sometimes boggy ground, takes around 10 to 12 hours to complete. From September to June, the region is covered in ice and snow. You need to be fit, well equipped, and careful. Injuries can happen, and in 2015, a walker sadly died.

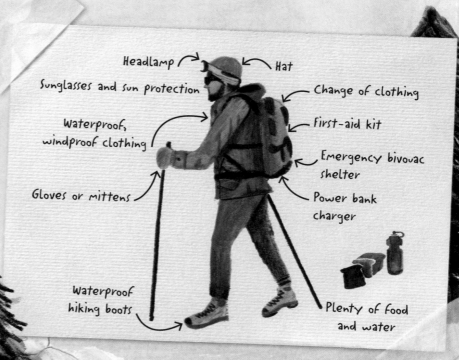

Headlamp

Hat

Sunglasses and sun protection

Change of clothing

Waterproof, windproof clothing

First-aid kit

Emergency bivouac shelter

Gloves or mittens

Power bank charger

Waterproof hiking boots

Plenty of food and water

# ROSS ICE SHELF

The Ross Ice Shelf is a floating ice block the size of France. It's in the sea off the coast of Antarctica – the coldest, windiest place on Earth. All ice shelves float over the sea. They are attached to glaciers that are moving over the land towards the coast. These glaciers feed the ice shelves. The Ross Ice Shelf is fed by more than five Antarctic glaciers.

The Ross Ice Shelf is the world's largest ice shelf. It floats over the Ross Sea. On the other side of Antarctica is the Ronne Ice Shelf, the world's second largest ice shelf.

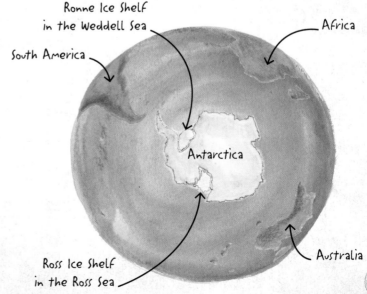

Ronne Ice Shelf
in the Weddell Sea

Africa

South America

Antarctica

Australia

Ross Ice Shelf
in the Ross Sea

About 90% of the Ross Ice Shelf is underwater.
The ice pushes out to sea at a rate of up to
3 m (10 ft) every day.

# FLOATING ICE CLIFFS

The biggest ice shelf in the world, in places the Ross Ice Shelf is 750 m (2,460 ft) deep (from its top to its bottom below the sea's surface). Its cliffs can reach up to 50 m (165 ft) above the water. The huge ice shelf forms a great barrier across the sea. The front of it is more than 600 km (370 miles) from side to side.

## Formation of icebergs

Sometimes cracks appear in the Ross Ice Shelf, and massive chunks of ice break off to form icebergs. Eventually, they move into warmer waters and melt. A giant iceberg that broke away in 2000 has since split into smaller and smaller pieces and drifted more than 10,000 km (6,600 miles) on the ocean currents.

A small block of floating ice is called a growler. Growlers are much smaller than icebergs.

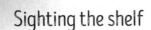

## Sighting the shelf

The Ross Ice Shelf was named after British explorer James Clark Ross, who first sighted it in 1841. It was later the starting point for an expedition to the South Pole led by Norwegian Roald Amundsen. In January 1911, he set up base camp at the Bay of Whales, a natural harbour in the shelf. He reached the South Pole on 14 December 1911.

Ross's ships, Erebus and Terror, had strengthened hulls for pushing through the pack ice over the Southern Ocean.

Weddell seal

IcePod

The IcePod is a system of instruments used to monitor how the Ross Ice Shelf is melting. It is mounted on a plane that flies over the ice shelf.

## Melting danger

The Ross Ice Shelf acts as a barrier, slowing the movement of the glaciers on land that feed into it. However, due to climate change, the Ross Ice Shelf might melt. Without it, the glaciers may start moving towards the coast five times faster than they are currently, and if they flow into the sea and melt, this will cause sea levels to rise.

Adélie penguins use the ice to rest on, so they are also threatened by climate change and rising temperatures.

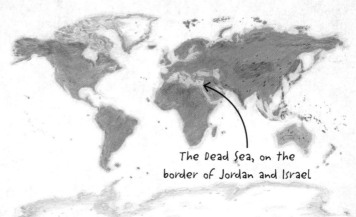

The Dead Sea, on the border of Jordan and Israel

# THE DEAD SEA

In the Judaean Desert, on the border of Jordan and Israel, lies the Dead Sea. Despite its name, it isn't actually a sea. It's a landlocked salt lake. The saltiest stretch of water on Earth, the Dead Sea is famously salty enough to float on. Salt crystallizes around its shores, creating beautiful shapes and formations.

These smooth pebbles are rounded crystals of halite (rock salt). Scattered on the lake's shores, they form by evaporation in the dry climate.

# LAKE FORMATION

At 430 m (1,410 ft) below sea level, the Dead Sea is the lowest point on the land areas of Earth (lower depths are found in oceans). It formed around 4 million years ago, when the Mediterranean Sea flooded the Jordan River Valley, creating a lagoon. Around 2 million years ago, movement of the Earth's crust made the land rise. This sealed off the lagoon from the sea, turning it into a lake.

## How the Dead Sea formed

Mediterranean Sea

Narrow lagoon in the Jordan River Valley

The Mediterranean Sea flooded the valley.

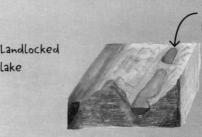

Land rose up

Landlocked lake

The land rose up due to movement of the Earth's crust. The lagoon became a landlocked lake.

Two smaller lakes

As the climate grew drier, the lake shrank, eventually becoming two smaller lakes.

Sea of Galilee

Dead Sea

One of the lakes is the Dead Sea. The other is the Sea of Galilee.

## Shrinking sea

In this desert area, water is diverted from the Jordan River that feeds the Dead Sea to be used for drinking and irrigation. Due to this, the lake level falls more than 1 m (3¼ ft) a year. As the Dead Sea shrinks, it leaves behind salty, dry land. Freshwater dissolves this unstable land, creating huge underground caverns. The roofs of the caverns can fall in, causing thousands of sinkholes to appear.

Between 1930 and 2016, the Dead Sea shrunk to almost half its size. Unstable, dry, salty land remains where it once was, and collapses, revealing sinkholes.

Deposits of salt build up on the Dead Sea's shores.

There are more than 35 minerals in the lake that create a variety of crystal formations.

## Super salty

Almost nine times saltier than the oceans, the Dead Sea is the saltiest body of water on Earth. Apart from tiny amounts of bacteria that have adapted to the conditions, plants and animals cannot survive in it, hence its name. The salt and other minerals in the Dead Sea create beautiful crystal formations.

The salt makes it impossible to sink in the water, but it's easy to float on the surface.

## Dead Sea tourists

For thousands of years, the Dead Sea has been popular with visitors from all over the world. They enjoy the amazing desert location, and the healing powers of the water and mud — the salt and other minerals are good for your skin. Hotels, resorts, and health spas are found along the lake shore.

Sea of Stars,
Maldives

# SEA OF STARS

In late summer in the Maldives, the night-time sea around the tropical island of Vaadhoo sparkles and shines as it laps against the shore. The water is full of microscopic plants that turn the inky black Indian Ocean into a mesmerizing sea of stars.

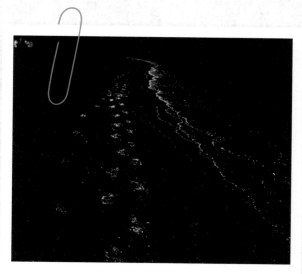

Take a night-time walk along the beach and leave behind glowing footprints in the sand.

# GLOW IN THE DARK

This incredible starry spectacle is called bioluminescence, and it's made by billions of tiny single-celled living things called phytoplankton. Phytoplankton are found in oceans and lakes. The light is created by a chemical reaction within them, activated by movement of the water. The light protects the phytoplankton by startling potential predators.

Phytoplankton are microscopic, single-celled living things (mostly plants, but they can have both plant and animal qualities).

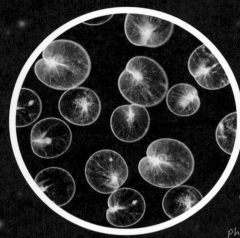

There are nearly 20 species of phytoplankton that light up.

Swimming in the glittering water at night is an experience you will never forget.

Kogelberg Biosphere Reserve, near Cape Town in South Africa, is another place where phytoplankton light up the night-time sea.

## More seas of stars

There are many places in the world where phytoplankton make the sea sparkle at night, including beaches in India, Thailand, Australia, Japan, Puerto Rico, South Africa, and the USA.

## Coral islands

The island of Vaadhoo is part of the Maldives, a country made up of around 1,300 coral islands and sandbanks. The islands have a hot, humid tropical monsoon climate that can reach temperatures of around 30°C (86°F). All the islands are flat and low-lying, nowhere more than 1.8 m (6 ft) above sea level.

Atolls

Island

There are some islands and many atolls in the Maldives. Atolls are islands of coral in the shape of a ring, with a lake of seawater in the middle called a lagoon.

## Reef life

Surrounding the islands are coral reefs, which teem with life. There are around 185 different species of coral and more than 1,000 species of marine animals, including sea turtles, giant clams, manta rays, and sharks.

Hawksbill sea turtle

Brain coral

Soft corals

Sea sponge

# GIANT'S CAUSEWAY

In Northern Ireland, thousands of stone pillars tumble dramatically from the cliffs. They form a causeway, said to have been used by giants. With a temperate climate, this area is often wet and windy, adding to the magnificent beauty of the rocky coast.

From overhead, you can see the shapes of the pillars. Many have five or six straight sides. This type of rock formation is called columnar jointing. It forms when liquid lava cools and becomes solid.

# COOL CAUSEWAY

Around 50 to 60 million years ago, massive volcanic activity forced molten basalt rock up through cracks in the ground. As this lava reached the sea, it cooled and hardened into columns. Pressure between the columns sculpted them into spectacular geometric shapes.

## How the Giant's Causeway formed

Around 60 million years ago, molten basalt lava poured out of cracks in the ground.

Column joints (cracks) formed, creating the column shapes in the basalt rock.

The basalt cooled quickly, cracking as it became solid (a little like the cracks in mud as it dries), forming the columns in the rock.

Erosion of the shore exposed the basalt cliffs.

Over time, glaciers, rising sea levels, coastal processes, and rain eroded the shore, exposing the Causeway columns.

## Giant myth

According to local folklore, the Giant's Causeway was built by Irish giant Fionn MacCumhaill (also known as Finn MacCool). A story tells how Fionn makes the causeway so he can cross the sea to Scotland, to fight his Scottish rival, Benandonner (who is threatening to take control of Ireland). But Benandonner is bigger than Fionn. So Fionn must play a trick on him to keep control of Ireland.

## MORE INCREDIBLE ROCK FORMATIONS

### Fingal's Cave, Scotland

Fingal's Cave is a sea cave on the island of Staffa, Scotland. Like the Giant's Causeway, its walls are made up of hexagonal columns of basalt rock.

## Giant features

Look out for these famous rock features as you explore the Giant's Causeway: pictured are the Camel and the Giant's Boot. Others include the Wishing Chair and the Pipe Organ.

The Camel: this rock is said to have once been a camel that carried Finn over long distances. It was later turned to stone.

Giant's Boot: this is said to be Finn's boot, lost as he fled, and believed to be a whopping size 93.5!

## Some animals of the Causeway Coast

From the side, the ocean sunfish has a round shape. It can grow to 1.8 m (6 ft) long.

Look out for the harbour seal popping its head out of the sea.

The largest member of the dolphin family, the orca lives in family groups called pods.

Seen all year round, the cormorant is a black seabird that dives to catch eels and fish.

The basking shark feeds on plankton and grows to a length of 6 to 8 m (20 to 26 ft).

## Cape Stolbchaty, Russia

Similar basalt columns can be seen at Cape Stolbchaty on Kunashir Island in Russia. The island is made up of four active volcanoes.

## Devil's Postpile, USA

The Devil's Postpile in California, USA, is made up of basalt columns up to 18 m (59 ft) tall. They look like a pile of tall posts, which is how the Postpile got its name.

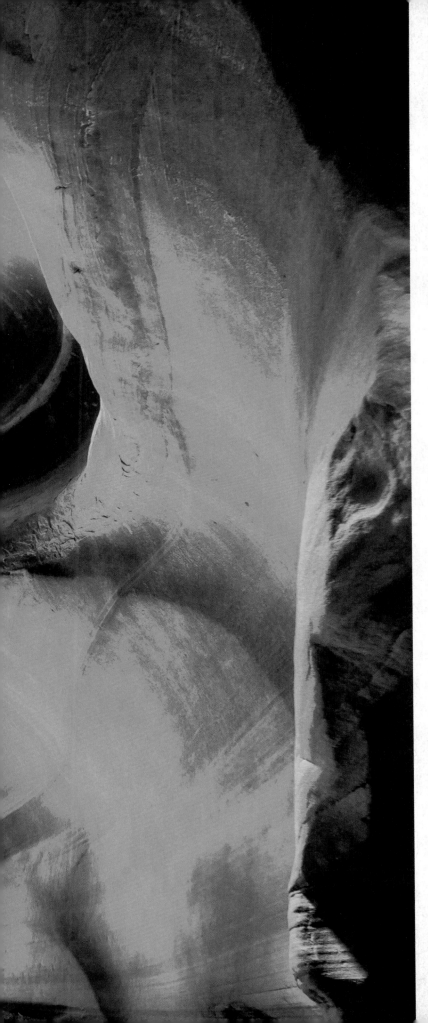

Antelope Canyon, USA

# ANTELOPE CANYON

A beam of sunlight shines through a crack in the ground, illuminating a stunning world of sandstone rock in swirling shades of orange and pink. This is Antelope Canyon in the arid shrublands of northern Arizona, USA. It's named after the antelopes that once grazed here.

The Heart is a spectacular feature in the shape of a heart inside Upper Antelope Canyon.

# SCULPTED SANDSTONE

Antelope Canyon is a slot canyon. This means it is a long, thin canyon, with steep rock walls. It was formed by rainwater and flash floods eroding the soft sandstone rock. Over millions of years, the water has carved out narrow passageways, with flowing, wave-like walls.

The different colours in the canyon's sandstone are caused by different minerals in the rock.

This view from above shows how slot canyons get their name. In places, Antelope Canyon is narrower than the width of two people.

At certain times, you can see a dramatic spotlight effect in The Crack (Upper Antelope Canyon), when light shines through a crack in the canyon's ceiling.

## The Crack and The Corkscrew

There are two parts to Antelope Canyon: Upper Antelope Canyon, known as The Crack, and Lower Antelope Canyon, known as The Corkscrew. Visitors usually start at Upper Antelope Canyon. Lower Antelope Canyon is longer and deeper and trickier to explore. To visit it, you'll need to climb several flights of ladders and stairs and not mind squeezing into a tight space.

## Sacred place for Navajo people

Antelope Canyon is located in Lake Powell Navajo Tribal Park on land that belongs to Navajo people. Navajo people are Indigenous people who live in the southwestern region of the USA. Many Navajo people live on a large reservation called the Navajo Nation, which has an independent government. Antelope Canyon is a sacred place for the Navajo, where they feel at harmony with nature. The canyon is treated with great respect.

Visitors to Antelope Canyon must be part of a tour led by a Navajo guide. Guides lead tours at Antelope Canyon and surrounding areas. Here, a guide is at nearby Monument Valley.

## Flash floods

The desert around the canyon is dry for most of the year, but flash floods can happen after heavy rain. The floodwater races through the canyon, and can prove deadly. In 1997, 11 visitors were killed. Since then, better flood safety measures have been installed, including permanent ladders (that won't be washed away), safety nets, and alarms.

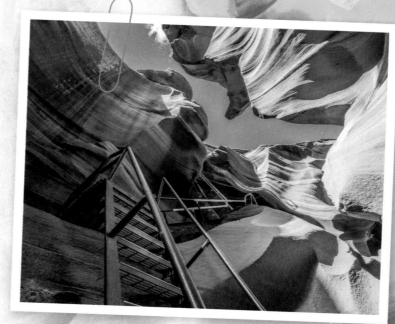

Ladder in Lower Antelope Canyon (known as The Corkscrew)

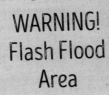

WARNING! Flash Flood Area

Fly Geyser,
USA

# FLY GEYSER

A truly eye-catching geyser stands on the edge of the Black Rock Desert in Nevada, USA. A geyser is a spring that shoots out hot water. Fly Geyser is located on the Hualapei Flats, an area known for its geothermal activity. Its spectacular colouring is down to a unique combination of rare minerals and heat-loving microscopic plants.

Fly Geyser stands around 3.7 m (12 ft) tall. The steam that rises from it, and its shooting jets of water can be seen from many kilometres around.

# GUSHING GEYSER

Springs form where underground water flows to the surface through cracks in the land. They can be hot or cold, and often create pools of water. A geyser is a type of hot spring that shoots out jets of water, from every few minutes to every few days. Geysers do form naturally, but Fly Geyser's spring formed after a well was drilled. Its cone then formed naturally.

The shooting water can reach a temperature of more than 93°C (200°F) — almost as hot as the water from a just-boiled kettle!

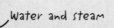

Water and steam

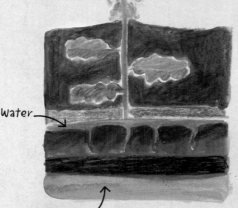

Water

Hot magma

## How geysers form

Magma heats underground water. The water turns to steam, which bursts to the surface, along with any water lying above it. After an eruption, the water seeps back through the ground again.

## Incredible colours

Minerals in the water, such as calcium carbonate, have solidified into cones and surrounding terraces. The hot, mineral-rich water provides a home for tiny plants, called green and red algae, that give the geyser its dazzling colours.

Fly Geyser cones

Wilson's phalaropes

## From well to spectacular geyser

In 1964, Fly Geyser was created by accident when a geothermal energy company drilled a second well on the site. Although they hit hot water, it wasn't hot enough to generate energy. They sealed the well, but this didn't stop the new geyser from erupting! Some spouts of hot water reach heights of around 1.5 m (5 ft).

See pp.121—123 for more geysers.

Flanked by mountains, the Black Rock Desert, Nevada, was a lake in prehistoric times, and is now a vast dry lakebed.

The algae are described as "thermophilic", which means that they love and thrive in hot, wet places, where other living things just couldn't survive. Here, they are seen under a microscope.

## Black Rock Desert

Fly Geyser is near to the Black Rock Desert. One of the flattest places on Earth, this desert is bone dry for most of the year. However, in spring, if enough rain falls, it floods with a few centimetres of water. Fairy shrimps lay millions of eggs in the mud. They hatch and grow before the water dries up, and are a vital food for flocks of migrating water birds, such as Wilson's phalaropes and American avocets.

American avocet

Grand Prismatic
Spring, USA

# GRAND PRISMATIC SPRING

The largest hot spring in Yellowstone National Park, USA, is the Grand Prismatic Spring. It's famous for its near-constant steam, scalding water, and dazzling display of rainbow colours. The colours are created by different types of heat-loving bacteria living around the spring's edges.

Since the water is always close to boiling point, the Grand Prismatic Spring constantly gives off a thick cloud of water vapour.

# HOT, HOT, HOT

A hot spring forms when water under the ground is heated by magma. The hot water rises to the surface, often creating a pool. At Grand Prismatic Spring, the water in the pool's centre is scorching hot, so very little can survive. But away from the centre, the pool cools, creating rings of different temperature water at the edges, where bacteria and algae are able to live.

The Grand Prismatic Spring's water seeps up from 37.5 m (121 ft) underground; in the centre, its temperature reaches 87°C (189°F).

## How hot springs form

Hot pool

Layers of rock

Heated water

Hot magma

The hot water rises through cracks in the ground, forming a hot spring and creating a pool at the surface.

Here, a colony of cyanobacteria (once classified as algae and commonly known as blue-green algae) is seen under a microscope.

## Rainbow colours

Different types of bacteria as well as algae live in the cooler rings of water away from the spring's centre. They have pigments that help them make food and protect them from sunlight. Each type of bacteria or algae contains different pigments that reflect only certain wavelengths of light. This gives the spring its multi-coloured edges. The central water is blue because it reflects the blue wavelength of light.

The spring's name comes from its prismatic colours (bright rainbow colours).

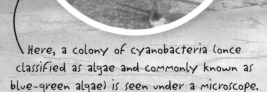
Bison

## Boiling Lake

High up in the mountains on the Caribbean island of Dominica, Boiling Lake lives up to its name. This hot spring's grey-blue water is heated by a volcano and bubbles away constantly, like water boiling in a giant saucepan.

Boiling Lake is usually surrounded by a thick cloud of steam and toxic gases, making it dangerous to approach.

After Tarawera erupted in 1886, craters formed and filled with water. After another eruption in 1917, Frying Pan Lake reached its present size.

## Frying Pan Lake

Bigger than four football pitches, Frying Pan Lake in New Zealand may be the world's largest hot spring. It lies in the crater of a volcano, Mount Tarawera.

See pp.153—155 and pp.161—163 for more hot springs.

The park contains different habitats — forests, grasslands, mountains, rivers, and lakes. It has mild, dry summers and cold, snowy winters.

In addition to its hot springs and geysers, Yellowstone National Park is famous for its wildlife.

Bighorn sheep

Moose

Chipmunks

Lake Natron,
Tanzania

# LAKE NATRON

One of the most inhospitable
environments on Earth, Lake Natron
lies in a branch of the East African Rift
Valley in Tanzania. Its water is hot,
extremely salty, and often coloured a
bright red by tiny bacteria that feed on
the salt. Swimming in the lake is strictly
off limits. The water is full of chemicals
that would seriously burn your skin.

Despite the harsh environment,
thousands of lesser flamingos
come to the lake to breed.

# HOT AND HARMFUL

Lake Natron is fed by the Ewaso Ng'iro River and also by mineral-rich hot springs that bring powerful chemicals. It's a big lake, around 60 km (37 miles) long, but it's less than 3 m (10 ft) deep. The temperature of the water is often higher than 40°C (104°F) — the temperature of a hot bath. The lake doesn't drain out to a sea or river, but its hot water evaporates, leaving salts and other minerals.

## How the lake water evaporates and becomes salty

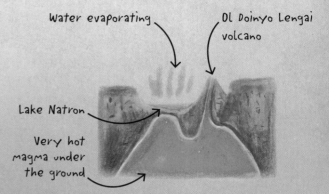

Water evaporating

Ol Doinyo Lengai volcano

Lake Natron

Very hot magma under the ground

Lake Natron is very salty. This is because hot magma under the ground heats the water so that it evaporates, leaving salts and other minerals. The hot, arid climate of the area aids the evaporation.

Lesser flamingos

In chemistry, substances like the salts in Lake Natron are called alkalis. Very strong alkalis, such as the ones found here, can burn skin.

## Flamingo friendly

For most plants and animals, Lake Natron is too hostile to call home. However, every few years, millions of lesser flamingos gather here to breed. Tough, leathery skin on their legs prevents them from getting burnt by the harmful water. They feed on lake algae and build their nests on small salt islands in the lake, safe from most predators.

## Volcano neighbour

The East African Rift Valley lies in a region where several plates of the Earth's crust meet. It is bordered by mountains and volcanoes. Some of the volcanoes are still active, including Ol Doinyo Lengai, a massive volcano that stands 2,962 m (9,718 ft) high and overlooks Lake Natron. When it erupts, lava spouts from small cones on the volcano's sides, as well as from the main crater.

Ol Doinyo Lengai erupts regularly, spouting out unusual lava that looks black when it is liquid, but turns white as it becomes solid.

The lake's water can be bright pink or red. The colour is caused by microscopic bacteria that thrive in the salty water.

As the lake's water evaporates, the salty ground dries and cracks.

## Turned to stone

Washed up on the lake shores are the bodies of animals, such as birds and bats, that look as if they have been turned to stone. These animals have been preserved by the salty water after crashing into the lake. One of the salts in the water was used by the ancient Egyptians to make their famous mummies — it's a salt called natron, from which the lake gets its name.

This bat's body was preserved by the salts and other minerals in the lake's water.

Deadvlei and
Sossusvlei, Namibia

# DEADVLEI AND SOSSUSVLEI

Surrounded by rusty-red sand dunes, the dry lakebeds of Deadvlei and Sossusvlei are two spectacular landscapes in the Namib Desert that were once marshes. Dead, dried-out trees, a thousand years old, stand trapped in the clay of Deadvlei.

The deep red colour of the dunes is rust, caused by iron in the sand.

The dead trees are acacia (camel thorn) trees. They are estimated to have lived more than 1,000 years ago.

# DEADVLEI

Thousands of years ago, the Tsauchab River flowed through the Deadvlei. But as the climate grew drier, the Deadvlei was cut off from the river by sand dunes. With no water, the area became a dry clay pan and the trees growing there died, but it was too dry for them to rot away. So they are still standing, scorched and blackened by the sun.

The dry, flat ground in clay and salt pans cracks into different patterns.

# SOSSUSVLEI

In the dry season, the salt and clay pan of Sossusvlei is bare and baked hard. After rain, the Tsauchab River flows into it, but quickly soaks into the ground. Every 10 years or so, the river floods after very heavy rain. The pan fills with water, forming a stunning, though temporary, turquoise-blue lake.

The Namib Desert stretches along the west coast of southern Africa. The largest part of it lies in Namibia.

Dead acacia (camel thorn) tree

Welwitschia mirabilis plant

## Dramatic dunes

Sand dunes form when the wind blows across the desert, piling up the sand into ridges. The shape and height of a dune depends on the speed and direction of the wind. The Namib Desert dunes can reach more than 350 m (1,145 ft), making them some of the tallest in the world.

**Windward side**
(the side of a dune where the wind is blowing and pushing sand up)

**Crest**

**Slip face**
(the side where the blown sand slips down)

The sand first starts to pile up around an obstruction such as wood debris.

The tallest dune in the Deadvlei is nicknamed Big Daddy. At 325 m (1,066 ft) high, it takes around two hours of climbing to reach the top.

## Namib Desert animals

Little rain falls in the Namib, but fog regularly rolls in from the sea. Some amazing plants and animals survive here by collecting moisture from the fog.

Water droplets are caught on the body of this fog-drinking beetle and drip down to its mouth.

The wide leaves of the Welwitschia mirabilis plant collect water from the fog by condensation. The leaves droop down, which means that the plant can water its own roots.

A gemsbok antelope gets moisture from the plants it eats. It survives the desert heat by breathing in and out quickly through its nose to cool down its blood.

Welwitschia mirabilis plant

Waitomo Glowworm Caves, New Zealand

# WAITOMO GLOWWORM CAVES

On New Zealand's North Island sits the village of Waitomo. At first glance, this village might seem like any other, but beneath it lies a vast network of limestone caves with a breathtaking feature that draws visitors from all over the world.

Temperature and carbon dioxide levels are regularly checked to manage and protect this magical environment.

The caves have spectacular displays of stalactites and stalagmites. These are rock formations made of minerals deposited by trickling rainwater.

# GHOSTLY BLUE GLOW

What makes the Waitomo Caves so special? As you venture into the caves, you'll see the walls and ceilings twinkling with tiny blueish lights. It's a breathtaking sight and draws many visitors. At the busiest time of the year, more than 2,000 people visit the caves every day.

## What causes the glow?

The tiny lights are produced by thousands of glowworms that hatch from eggs laid on the cave walls. The glowworms are larvae (young insects). They grow into a species of fungus gnat that is only found in New Zealand. Inside a glowworm's abdomen, chemicals react together to give off a blue glow.

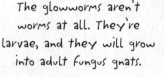

The glowworms aren't worms at all. They're larvae, and they will grow into adult fungus gnats.

### Larvae

At first, the larvae are 3 to 5 mm (1/8 to 1/4 in) long. They grow to 30 to 40 mm (1 1/4 to 1 1/2 in).

### Pupae

After several months, the larvae spin silk cocoons around their bodies.

### Fungus gnat

While in their cocoons, the larvae are changing, and after about two weeks, they emerge as adult gnats.

## MORE INCREDIBLE CAVES TO EXPLORE

### Orda Cave, Russia

One of the longest underwater caves in the world, the Orda Cave's crystal-clear waters make it a dream destination for scuba divers.

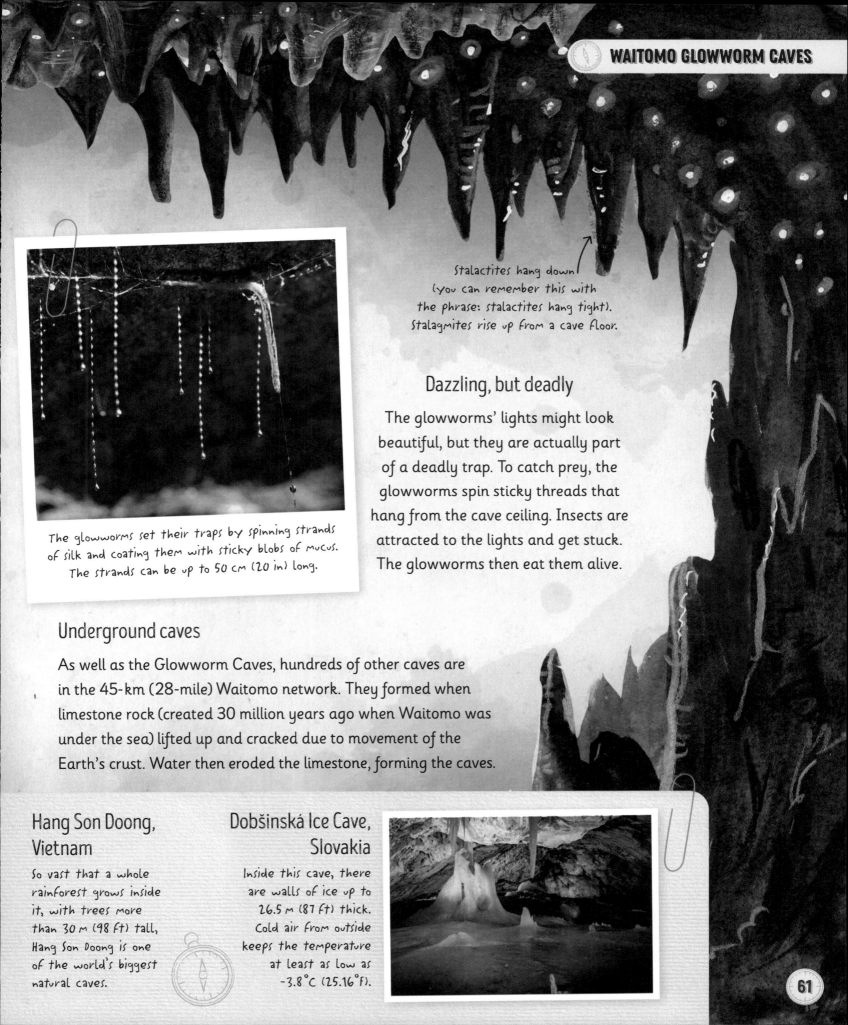

Stalactites hang down
(you can remember this with
the phrase: stalactites hang tight).
Stalagmites rise up from a cave floor.

The glowworms set their traps by spinning strands
of silk and coating them with sticky blobs of mucus.
The strands can be up to 50 cm (20 in) long.

## Dazzling, but deadly

The glowworms' lights might look beautiful, but they are actually part of a deadly trap. To catch prey, the glowworms spin sticky threads that hang from the cave ceiling. Insects are attracted to the lights and get stuck. The glowworms then eat them alive.

## Underground caves

As well as the Glowworm Caves, hundreds of other caves are in the 45-km (28-mile) Waitomo network. They formed when limestone rock (created 30 million years ago when Waitomo was under the sea) lifted up and cracked due to movement of the Earth's crust. Water then eroded the limestone, forming the caves.

## Hang Son Doong, Vietnam

So vast that a whole rainforest grows inside it, with trees more than 30 m (98 ft) tall, Hang Son Doong is one of the world's biggest natural caves.

## Dobšinská Ice Cave, Slovakia

Inside this cave, there are walls of ice up to 26.5 m (87 ft) thick. Cold air from outside keeps the temperature at least as low as -3.8°C (25.16°F).

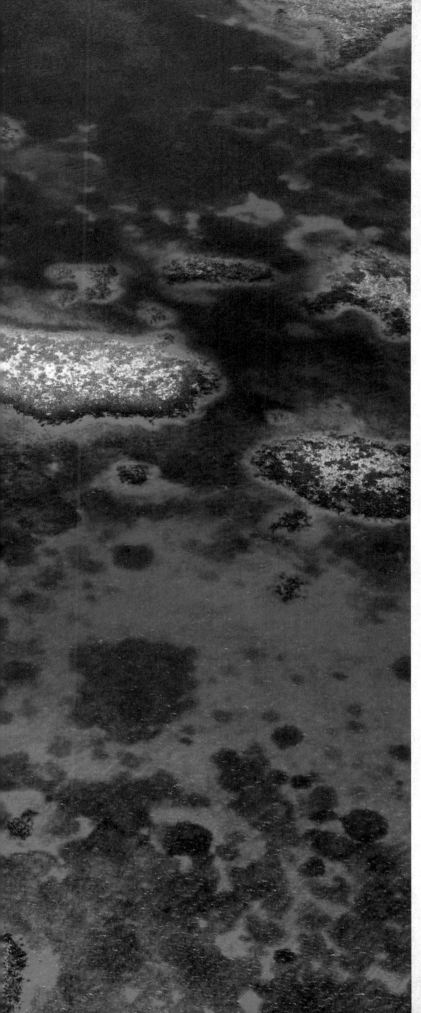

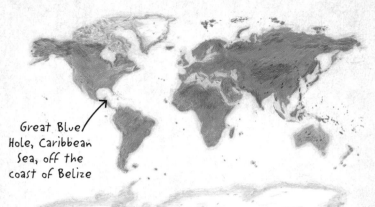

Great Blue Hole, Caribbean Sea, off the coast of Belize

# GREAT BLUE HOLE

At the centre of a coral reef in the Caribbean Sea sits an almost perfectly round dark circle. It stands out so much from the turquoise water, it looks as if there's a hole in the sea. And in fact, that's exactly what it is.

At around 300 m (1,000 ft) across, and 125 m (400 ft) deep, the Great Blue Hole is the world's largest sinkhole.

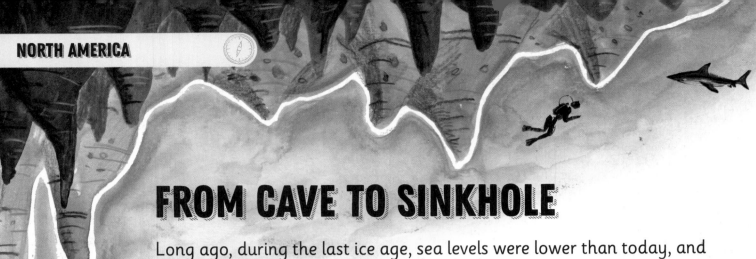

# FROM CAVE TO SINKHOLE

Long ago, during the last ice age, sea levels were lower than today, and the Great Blue Hole was on land. It was an underground cave, carved out of limestone. Eventually, its ceiling collapsed. Geologists aren't sure why, but it's most likely that, as ice melted and sea levels rose, weathering and erosion caused by the sea led to the collapse. The sea then filled the hole with water.

## How the sinkhole formed

Cave

Land (rock)

Sea levels rose, and during this time the cave's ceiling collapsed. The reason for this is not known for certain, but it was probably due to weathering and erosion caused by the sea.

Around 18,000 years ago, the Great Blue Hole was an underground cave.

Sea

Stalagmites remain at the base. This was once the floor of the cave.

Over time, the remaining part of the cave filled with water, forming the Great Blue Hole in the sea.

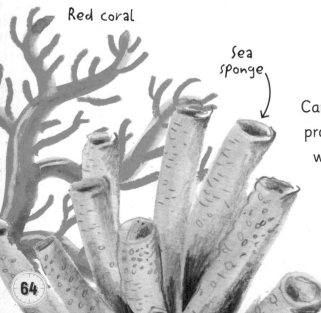

Red coral

Sea sponge

Brain coral

## Life in the depths

In the tropical climate of the Caribbean Sea, the Great Blue Hole provides a rich habitat for marine wildlife, from parrotfish and reef sharks, to sea turtles, groupers, butterfly fish, and some 150 species of coral.

Sea turtle

## Diving deep

The only way to get up close to the Great Blue Hole is by scuba diving. It is one of the top diving destinations in the world. Divers come to explore the amazing clear waters and take in the sights. But it is only safe for experienced divers with advanced-level qualifications.

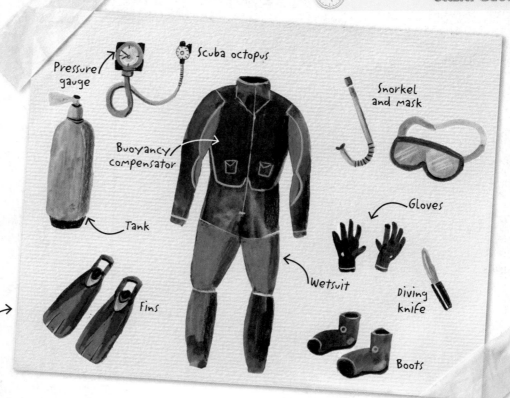

Pressure gauge

Scuba octopus

Buoyancy compensator

Snorkel and mask

Gloves

Tank

Wetsuit

Diving knife

Fins

Boots

Scuba divers need special equipment to explore the Great Blue Hole safely.

Ocean explorer Jacques Cousteau made the Great Blue Hole famous. In 1972, a TV show followed his voyage to the sinkhole.

## Evidence in the rocks

One of the reasons scientists know that the Great Blue Hole was once above sea level is that it contains stalactites and stalagmites. These are mineral deposits found in caves on land. It is not possible for stalactites and stalagmites to form underwater. Learn more about stalactites and stalagmites on pp.60–61.

Caribbean reef shark
(not considered dangerous)

Stalagmite

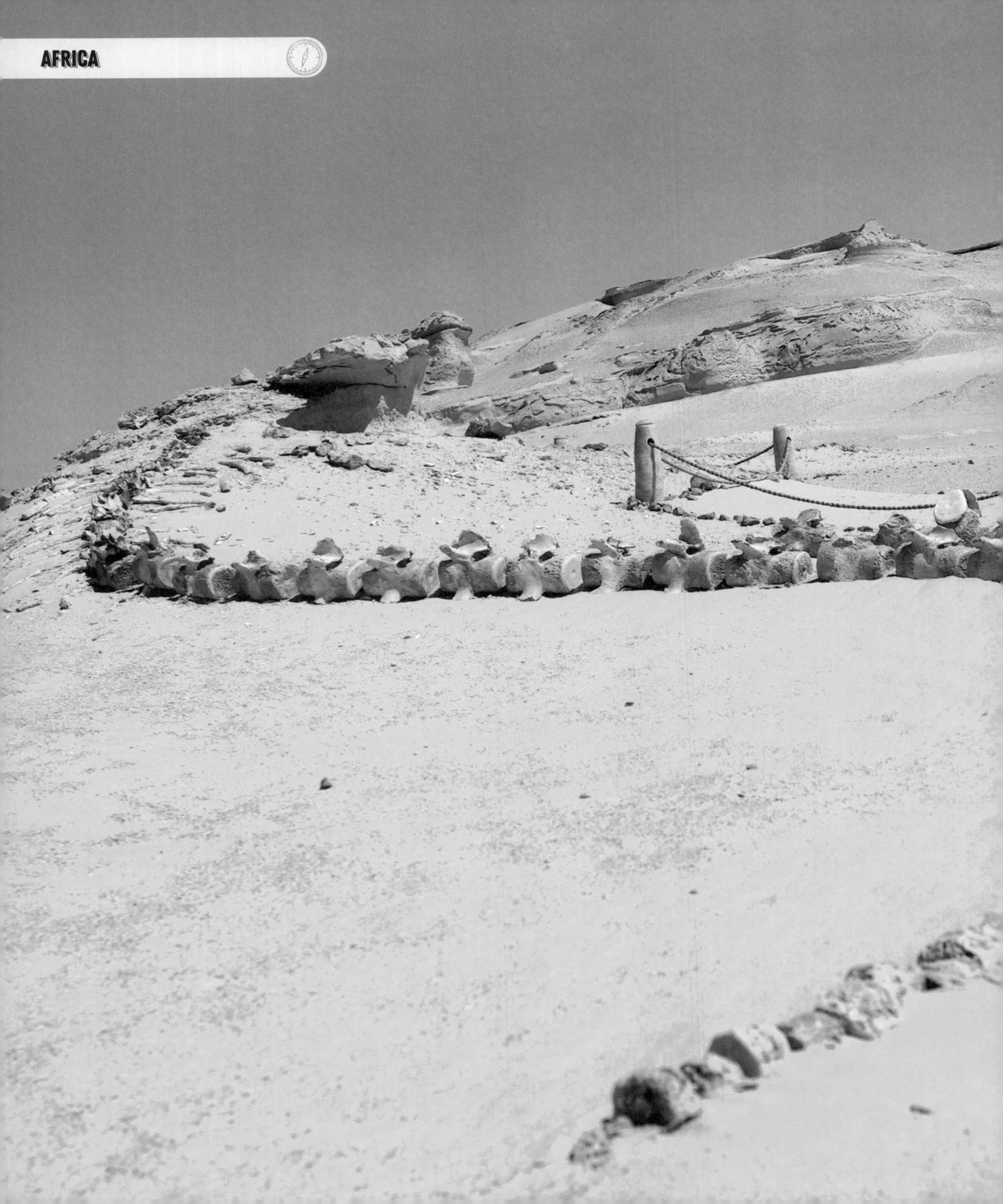

Valley of the
Whales, Egypt

# VALLEY OF THE WHALES

In a valley in Egypt's Western Desert lies an extraordinary collection of fossils. They are the giant bones of prehistoric whales that lived 37 million years ago. Called "Wadi Al-Hitan" (Valley of the Whales), the site has provided fossil scientists with the answer to a long-standing mystery — did whales ever live on land?

The massive skull of a prehistoric whale,
Basilosaurus, found at Wadi Al-Hitan.

# OASIS OF BONES

Although Wadi Al-Hitan is now desert, it was once covered in a shallow, tropical sea. Most of the whale bones found here belong to two species – Basilosaurus and Dorudon. There are also bones from turtles, crocodiles, catfish, and sharks. The skeletons are remarkably well preserved, even down to broken teeth and the remains of fish inside their stomachs.

### Walking whales

In the 1980s, US fossil scientist Philip Gingerich made an amazing discovery at Wadi Al-Hitan. While excavating a Basilosaurus skeleton, he found the first known whale knee bone. Later, he found back leg, feet, and ankle bones, together with a complete set of tiny toes, proving that whales once walked on land.

Human adult

Knee

Basilosaurus

Whale bones

Some of the bones in the spine are as big as logs.

In 2015, the first complete Basilosaurus skeleton was discovered at Wadi Al-Hitan. To protect it, the 18-m (59-ft) long skeleton is now displayed in a newly built museum at the site.

# How whales developed over time

50 million years ago

### Pakicetus

One of the earliest whale ancestors, Pakicetus lived on land and walked on all fours.

50 to 48 million years ago

### Ambulocetus

A whale-like predator, Ambulocetus was comfortable living on land and in water.

46 to 47 million years ago

### Rodhocetus

This whale ancestor had short legs. Its feet may have been webbed for swimming.

34 to 40 million years ago

### Basilosaurus

A giant sea creature, Basilosaurus had a long, slender, eel-like body and a narrow snout.

40 to 33 million years ago

### Dorudon

Dorudon had a shape similar to a modern whale. Its teeth were sharp and dagger-like.

34 million years ago

### Humpback whale

Over time, modern whales developed. Some, such as the humpback, grew sieve-like parts in their mouths (in place of teeth) for straining food from the sea. Other modern whales still have teeth.

## Taking to water

Fossil scientists think that the first whales lived around 55 million years ago along the coast. In search of food, they ventured deeper and deeper into the sea. Over millions of years, their front limbs became flippers and the tips of their tails broadened for swimming. Later, in place of teeth, some grew baleen — filtering parts inside their mouths for straining food from the ocean.

A fennec fox's oversized ears help to keep it cool by drawing heat away from its body.

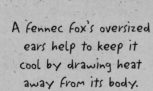

fennec fox

## Desert features

Millions of years after the whales walked here, Wadi Al-Hitan now lies in scorching, sandy desert, with very little water for kilometres around. Even so, animals such as North African jackals, dorcas gazelles, and fennec foxes have adapted to life in this hostile habitat.

Dorcas gazelle

Zhangjiajie
Mountains,
China

# ZHANGJIAJIE MOUNTAINS

The Zhangjiajie Mountains in northwest China are made up of 3,000 giant rocky pillars that jut into the sky from the forest floor. Their almost vertical sides are dotted with green trees and shrubs, and their tops are often hidden by cloud. This unique landscape has inspired sci-fi films.

The mountains look magical in winter under a rare coating of snow.

# PEAKY PILLARS

At a height of 1,262 m (4,140 ft), the tallest pinnacles tower above the others. Evergreen trees and bushes cling to their sides and peaks. The climate is subtropical monsoon – mostly warm and humid, with rainfall throughout the year, and temperatures up to around 35°C (95°F) and as low as 0°C (32°F). The pillars and the forest are part of the Zhangjiajie National Forest Park.

Near the Zhangjiajie Mountains is Heaven's Door, a 130-m (425-ft) high, cavernous gap in the rock.

## How the Zhangjiajie Mountains formed

Ocean

Quartz sandstone rock formed under the water.

The land lifted up above sea level.

Cracks

Quartz sandstone

River ← Pillar-like mountains

Water

The mountains are capped with ancient quartz sandstone, up to 500 m (1,640 ft) thick.

Some 300 million years ago, this region was an ocean.

The land lifted up due to movement of the Earth's crust, creating cracks in the rock.

Rivers, winter ice, and weathering widened and eroded the cracks in the rocks, leaving behind the pillar-like Zhangjiajie Mountains.

## Mountain carving

The pillar-like mountains are made of quartz sandstone rock (sandstone that is made up mostly of quartz). A very long time ago, this region was part of the ocean, and the quartz sandstone formed under the water. Due to movement of the Earth's crust, the land lifted up, creating cracks in the rock. Over millions of years, rivers, ice, and weathering widened the cracks and eroded the rocks, carving the pillar-like mountains.

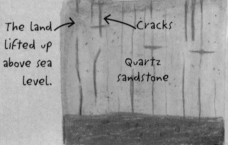

## Park wildlife

Apart from its famous pillars, Zhangjiajie National Forest Park has thick forests, deep valleys, rivers, lakes, and caves. These provide habitats for many plants and animals, including the Chinese chestnut tree (native to China) and the Chinese giant salamander, which is critically endangered and now protected by law.

The Chinese giant salamander is the largest amphibian in the world and can reach lengths of 1.8 m (6 ft).

**MORE SIGHTS TO SEE AT ZHANGJIAJIE MOUNTAINS**

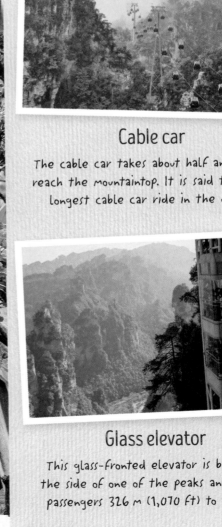

### Mountain road

The winding road that goes up the steep mountains has 99 sharp bends, with sheer drops over the side.

### Cable car

The cable car takes about half an hour to reach the mountaintop. It is said to be the longest cable car ride in the world.

### Glass elevator

This glass-fronted elevator is built into the side of one of the peaks and carries passengers 326 m (1,070 ft) to the top.

Lake Hillier,
Australia

# LAKE HILLIER

On Middle Island, off the south coast
of Western Australia, sits a stunning
lake. Its water is bright bubble-gum pink,
in contrast to the turquoise blue of the
ocean nearby. The water is safe to swim
in, although the lake is very tricky
to reach if you fancy a dip.

A thick forest surrounds Lake
Hillier, where many eucalyptus
and paperbark trees grow.

Paperbark
trees

# TRADITIONAL CUSTODIANS

Wudjari people are the traditional custodians (owners) of the land here. They have known about the lake for centuries. There are Wudjari heritage sites nearby, such as rock shelters and places for ceremonies. The name Hillier doesn't come from the Wudjari people (a British explorer who came here in 1802 named the lake Hillier after a member of his ship's crew).

There are heritage sites across Australia belonging to First Australians. This picture is from a Ngurrara rock shelter in the Kimberley region, northern Western Australia. It depicts a fish hunt.

### In the pink

Lake Hillier is a salt lake. It is 600 m (1,968 ft) long. Its pink colour is thought to be caused by the particular mix of micro-algae (tiny plant-like things) and other single-celled organisms (tiny living things) that thrive in its salty water. There are salt-loving organisms in every salt lake on Earth.

Salt dries into crystals on the lake's shores. The water stays permanently pink, even if it's taken out of the lake.

## MORE PINK LAKES TO EXPLORE

### Lake Retba, Senegal

In the warm, semi-arid climate of Senegal, Lake Retba is at its pinkest between November and June — the dry season. Visit then, at around midday, to see it at its best, and enjoy a swim.

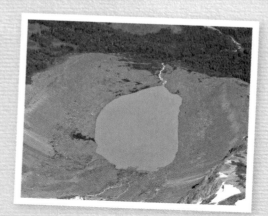

## Lake life

Algae is the only living thing that can survive in the lake itself. But the lake is part of a much larger nature reserve that includes more than 100 islands and coral reefs off Western Australia's south coast. The islands are important breeding sites for seabirds, such as shearwaters and penguins, and mammals, such as sea lions and fur seals.

flesh-footed shearwater

The islands have a Mediterranean climate with hot, dry summers and mild, wet winters.

Australian sea lions

New Zealand fur seal

Little penguins

Cape Barren geese

## Dusty Rose Lake, Canada

Dusty Rose Lake sits high up on a mountain. Minerals in the glacier meltwater that feeds this lake cause its pastel-pink colour. The lake is safe to swim in.

## Sasyk-Sivash Lagoon, Russia

This pink lake looks lovely, but it smells terrible. Despite this, you can swim here. Workers extract tonnes of rare pink salt from the water. It is sold around the world.

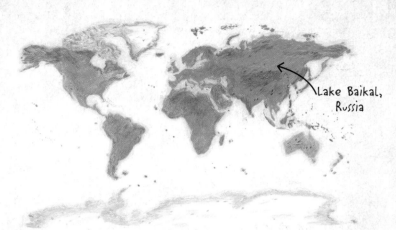

Lake Baikal, Russia

# LAKE BAIKAL

Deep in the remote wilderness of Siberia, Russia, is Lake Baikal, the oldest, deepest, and most voluminous freshwater lake in the world. In winter, bubbles of methane gas freeze in the clear water. In summer, take a dip, although the lake is still chilly! The region's cold temperate climate helps to create the perfect environment for some unique wildlife, such as a deer with fangs and a freshwater seal.

The lake is home to the Baikal seal, called "nerpa" by the local people. It's one of the very few seal species that can live in fresh water.

# ABOUT BAIKAL

Covering some 31,500 sq km (12,120 sq miles), Lake Baikal is bigger than Belgium. By volume, it is the largest freshwater lake in the world, containing around one-fifth of all freshwater on Earth. The deepest lake on the planet, it plunges to a maximum depth of 1,620 m (5,320 ft).

Lake Baikal is deep enough for five Eiffel Towers to stand on top of each other!

## Lake history

Lake Baikal is a long, curved, crescent-shaped lake surrounded by mountains. It was formed around 20 to 25 million years ago in an ancient rift valley where two plates of the Earth's crust are slowly pulling apart. The rift is still growing wider by about 2 cm ($^3/_4$ in) a year, and this movement triggers earthquakes every few years. Learn more about rift valleys on p.12.

Methane bubbles form in the lake when bacteria (from decomposing leaves and creatures) releases methane gas. These bubbles rise to the surface of the lake and in winter they freeze.

In February and March, the ice covering the lake is thick enough to drive over. It can be up to 2 m ($6^1/_2$ ft) thick.

The Buryat decorate tree branches and poles with colourful ribbons representing prayers.

The traditional robes of the Buryats are called deels. They can be made from wool, cotton, or silk. In winter, layered clothing protects the Buryats from the cold.

## People of Baikal

The Buryats live to the south and east of Lake Baikal and on Olkhon Island (see below). The lake is sacred to them. They believe that their gods and spirits live there. Their traditional clothes are often brightly coloured. The colours have special meanings: black stands for Earth, blue for the heavens (upper worlds), and red for the lower worlds.

Three Brothers Rocks

## Islands in the lake

Around 27 islands lie in Lake Baikal, including Three Brothers Rocks. Legend says that these rocks were once three brothers, but they were turned to stone by their father. The largest island in Lake Baikal is Olkhon Island, the third largest lake island in the world. It has a dramatic landscape of steep mountains, thick forests, island lakes, and patches of semi-desert.

## Baikal wildlife

Lake Baikal is home to more than 2,500 species of animals and 1,000 species of plants. Around 80% of these are found nowhere else in the world. The most famous are the nerpa (Baikal seal), golomyanka (Baikal oilfish), and omul (a salmon species), but more than half the fish in the lake are unique, together with molluscs, crustaceans, flatworms, snails, and sponges. Many other animals live in the mountains and forests around the lake.

The omul is a species of salmon. It's caught in large numbers for food, but overfishing is putting the species at risk of extinction.

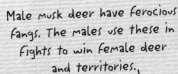

Male musk deer have ferocious fangs. The males use these in fights to win female deer and territories.

Siberian roe deer are small, graceful animals that live in forests around the lake. In winter, they gather in herds and migrate further up the valley.

Eurasian wolves live in large packs that cooperate with one another to hunt deer, reindeer, and wild boar.

Eurasian brown bears have thick fur for surviving the cold in the mountain forests. They mostly eat berries, grass, and insects.

## Baikal in danger

Today, Lake Baikal's unique environment faces many dangers. Sewage and chemical run-off from farms and factories pollute the lake and cause toxic algae to bloom. Overfishing threatens fish populations. Tourists leave behind rubbish. Environmental agencies have had some successes; in 2013, a pulp and paper mill was shut down and plans for an oil pipeline close to the shore were stopped.

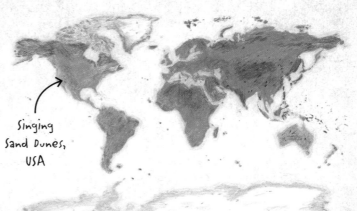

Singing
Sand Dunes,
USA

# SINGING SAND DUNES

In remote Eureka Valley, California, USA, stunning sand dunes rise from a dry lake bed. In this windswept, desert landscape, listen carefully as you climb the dunes – the sand may start to sing. The Eureka Dunes are some of the tallest in North America. They are mostly long and narrow, forming ridges, side by side. Others are star-shaped.

The dunes are the tallest in California and would tower over the Great Pyramid.

The Great Pyramid,
120 m (400 ft)

Eureka Dunes,
more than 210 m (700 ft)

# EUREKA HABITAT

The dunes lie near the end of Eureka Valley, where windblown sand collects (see p.57 for how sand dunes form). The habitat is harsh. But wildlife here is helped by the nearby mountains, which capture rain. This seeps into the sand, and the dunes hold the water, like a sponge.

Last Chance Mountains

## The sides of a sand dune

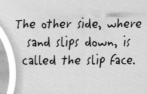

**Windward side**

The side of a dune where the wind is blowing and pushing sand up is called the windward side.

The other side, where sand slips down, is called the slip face.

**Slip face**

## Dune plants

Some plants are able to grow in the sand, including rare species found only on the Eureka Dunes.

Eureka dunegrass grows only on the Eureka Dunes. It's found high up on the dune slopes and uses its thick roots to anchor itself in the sand. It has stiff spines on the tips of its leaves to stop it being eaten.

The Eureka Dunes evening primrose is found only on the Eureka Dunes. It stays under the sand until it rains. Then it grows very quickly. Its white flowers open at night to attract pollinators, such as moths.

The freckled milkvetch is found across western North America. It is covered in silvery hairs that reflect away excess heat and save moisture. It forms hummocks on the dunes.

Great Basin gopher snake

Chuckwalla
(a type of lizard)

## Incredible singing sand

If you climb a Eureka dune and push the sand down the slope with your feet, or if the wind blows sand down a slope's side, you may hear an amazing booming sound, like a small aircraft or a low note of a pipe organ. This happens because the conditions here allow the grains of sand to slip and slide against each other, which creates the sound.

Not all dunes in the world sing. But at Eureka, when the sand is very dry, conditions are perfect: the sand grains are loosely packed, clean, and the right size, and the slopes are a good size, too.

Trekking here is tough, but worth it for the dramatic scenery.

## Dune animals

As well as specially adapted plants, the dunes are home to animals such as snakes, lizards, and beetles. Darkling beetles burrow into the sand during the day to escape the heat and predators.

Darkling beetle

## Death Valley

The Eureka Dunes are found in a remote part of Death Valley National Park. The park's habitats range from some of the hottest and driest environments in North America to snow-covered mountains and flower-filled meadows. More than 1,000 species of plants and 440 species of animals make their home in the park, some of which are found nowhere else in the world.

The kit fox is a small fox that lives in Death Valley. Its very large ears help it to listen out for prey and they release heat to keep it cool.

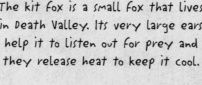

Kit fox

87

Tsingy de Bemaraha,
Madagascar

# TSINGY DE BEMARAHA

In the west of Madagascar, razor-sharp rocks rise up from the ground like a forest of pointy needles. Each one is a "tsingy" — a Malagasy word that roughly translates to "where you cannot go barefoot". Since the rocks are sharp enough to cut through the soles of walking boots, the name couldn't be more fitting.

There are damp caves at the base of the steep-sided tsingys and sun-beaten peaks at the top.

# CANYON CARVING

The tsingys are formed from slabs of easily dissolvable limestone rock. Geologists think these rocks were mainly dissolved and shaped by groundwater and rain, which seeped into them, creating the needles, as well as the caves, canyons, and tunnels. There are only a few places in the world with this type of landscape.

## How the tsingys formed

Sea    Land moved up    Limestone

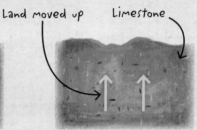

Limestone

Around 200 million years ago, this area was an ocean. A bed of very pure limestone rock formed under the water.

Later, movement of the Earth's crust caused the land (with the bed of limestone) to rise out of the sea. The land was revealed further as sea levels fell.

Rain

Limestone started to dissolve

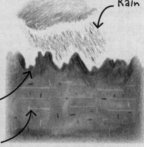

Groundwater

Groundwater

Over millions of years, groundwater (water in the ground) dissolved and shaped the limestone, forming deep, large caves in the rock. Rain helped to dissolve the very top of the rock.

As time went on, the roofs of the large caves were eroded, forming deep canyons (very narrow, steep-sided gorges). Today, groundwater and rain continue to dissolve and sharpen the rock features.

It's very difficult to get around the tsingys, and large parts are unexplored.

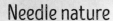

## Needle nature

The Tsingy de Bemaraha and its forest are a protected nature reserve. This area has a warm but dry tropical climate, and unique wildlife. Scientists regularly find new wildlife species. The rainy season lasts from October to April. During the rest of the year, it's dry, and plants find clever ways to survive.

Pachypodium lamerei (a flowering plant) stores water in its stem, and its spines collect moisture from fog.

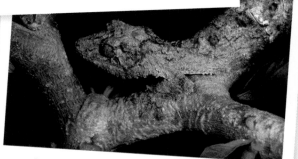

By day, the leaf-tailed gecko rests on branches, perfectly hidden by its superb camouflage. At night, it hunts insects.

Baobab trees store water in their bulging trunks.

Some tsingys can reach 100 m (330 ft) in height.

## Leaping lemurs

Decken's sifaka is one of Madagascar's largest lemurs. With its powerful back legs, it cruises the top of the tsingys, looking for leaves and fruit to eat. Thick pads of skin protect the sifaka's feet, helping it to land safely among the sharp splinters of stone.

The sifaka can leap distances of up to 30 m (100 ft).

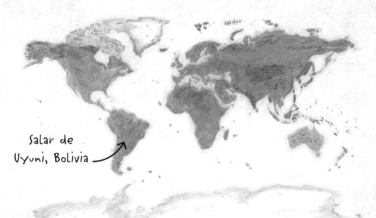

Salar de
Uyuni, Bolivia

# SALAR DE UYUNI

Stretching away towards the horizon,
Salar de Uyuni in Bolivia is a vast,
glistening-white salt flat. Featured in many
sci-fi films, this otherworldly landscape
is a salt desert. The salt flats are dry in
the desert's dry season. On the few days
when it rains in the short rainy season,
the salt flats are briefly covered in
a very thin layer of water.

The expansive salt crust beautifully reflects the
scenery when wet. It can be up to 10 m (33 ft) thick,
and when wet or dry, visitors can walk and drive on it.

# MIRROR LAKE

At more than 10,000 sq km (3,681 sq miles), Salar de Uyuni is the largest salt flat, or playa, in the world. It was left behind when prehistoric lakes evaporated around 40,000 years ago. It is one of the flattest places on Earth. In the rainy season from January to March, if a thin layer of water covers it, the salt flat transforms into a giant mirror.

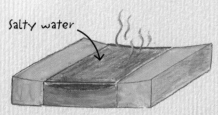

## How salt flats form

Salty water

Salt flats form in climates where the rate of water evaporation exceeds the rate of rainfall.

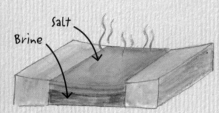

Salt

Brine

As the salty water (brine) dries up, the previously dissolved salt is left behind, with brine remaining underneath it.

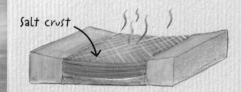

Salt crust

The solid salt becomes a crust that gets thicker and thicker as the evaporation process continues.

The pattern of polygons (many-sided shapes) is a result of how the salt crystals in the crust grow and crack in the dry season.

The shapes can be 1 to 4 m (3 to 13 ft) across.

Salty mud and brine

## Salar harvest

Underneath the Salar's salty crust is a pool of salty mud and brine. Lithium carbonate, a type of salt found in the brine, is commercially extracted. Lithium is used in batteries for mobile phones, laptops, and electric cars.

## Salt hotels

If you're visiting the Salar de Uyuni and want a quirky place to stay, check in at the Palacio de Sal (Palace of Salt). This incredible hotel is made from around a million blocks of Salar salt. It even has a salt golf course. To keep it looking fresh, it is rebuilt every 15 years.

Inside the hotel, the tables, chairs, and beds are all made from blocks of salt.

Isla Incahuasi (House of the Inca) is an island in the middle of the salt desert. It was once a stopping-off point for the Inca people as they crossed the salt flat. It is famous for its giant cacti, some of which are hundreds of years old.

The giant cacti grow slowly, at a rate of 1 cm (1/2 in) a year. Most are more than 2 m (6 1/2 ft) tall. Some can reach 10 m (33 ft)!

## Flamingo habitat

The Salar is an important breeding site for three species of South American flamingos: James, Andean, and Chilean. The birds arrive in November. They are adapted for feeding in salty lakes — they lose excess salt through glands near their nostrils.

Ha Long Bay,
Vietnam

# HA LONG BAY

Thousands of limestone islands and rocky outcrops are dotted like jewels in the emerald-green waters of beautiful Ha Long Bay in northeast Vietnam. In the bay's tropical climate, magnificent rainforests grow on the islands and coral reefs teem with hundreds of species of coral, fish, molluscs, and crustaceans.

Boats carry visitors on guided tours of the fantastical bay.

# ABOUT A BAY

Ha Long Bay has around 2,000 limestone islands that are between 50 to 100 m (160 to 330 ft) above sea level. Around 340 to 240 million years ago, all this area was underwater. Over time, it became exposed due to the Earth's crust moving and lifting, and sea levels falling. The land was then eroded by waves and rain, dissolving and shaping the limestone rock. Some of the islands are named after their unusual shapes, such as Cho Da (Stone Dog) Islet and Con Coc (Toad) Islet.

The ceiling of Hang Dau Go can reach up to 25 m (82 ft) in places. Sunlight streams in through the opening, allowing mosses to grow inside the cave.

## Wooden Stakes Cave

Some of the islands have huge caves. The largest is Hang Dau Go (Wooden Stakes Cave), which has three large chambers with stalactites, stalagmites, and even a freshwater lake (see pp.60–61 for more about stalactites and stalagmites). The cave is named after the remains of sharp wooden posts placed in the water in the 13th century by the Vietnamese military to sink invaders' ships.

Lizards, bats, birds, and monkeys make their homes in the rainforest habitat, which has a tropical climate of hot, wet summers and drier, cooler winters.

Hawk

## Where the dragon descends into the sea

The name "Ha Long" is Vietnamese for "descending dragon". Legend tells how a dragon and her children came down from heaven to save the local people from an attack. The dragon breathed out fire, emeralds, and jade, and the jewels became the islands in the bay.

Cat Ba Island is home to the white-headed langur, one of the rarest monkeys in the world.

## People of the bay

Around 1,600 people live in and around the bay, in small fishing villages. Their houses float on wooden platforms in the water. Next to the houses are large, floating wooden frames covered in nets, where the villagers farm fish for a living. Villagers also offer accommodation and boat tours to tourists visiting the bay.

Fish farms are next to the brightly painted houses in this floating fishing village in Ha Long Bay.

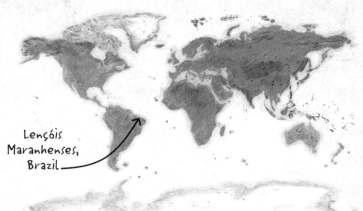

Lençóis
Maranhenses,
Brazil

# LENÇÓIS MARANHENSES

Along the northeast coast of Brazil lies the Lençóis Maranhenses – a rippling landscape of shimmering white sand dunes with deep pools of water in the dips in between. From the air, the dunes look like bedsheets billowing in the wind, and that is how they got their name: "Lençóis" means "bedsheets" in Portuguese.

The areas between the dunes form small troughs (dips) that fill with rainwater in the wet season. In the dry season, the pools evaporate again.

# BILLOWING BEDSHEETS

Two rivers flow through the Lençóis Maranhenses, carrying thousands of tonnes of sand. They dump most of it near the sea. In the dry season, strong winds blow the sand back inland, piling it up into crescent-shaped dunes, with small valleys between them, forming the Lençóis Maranhenses (find out more about sand dune formation on p.57).

Flocks of scarlet ibis fly to the dunes to feed. They use their long bills to probe for shellfish in the sandy lagoons.

## Dunes and lagoons

Despite its sand dunes, the Lençóis Maranhenses isn't a desert. It has a tropical climate – warm all year, with a wet season from January to June, and a dry season from July to December. In the wet season, the dips between the dunes fill with rainwater up to 3 m (10 ft) deep. A layer of impermeable rock under the sand stops the water from soaking away. The pools evaporate when the dry season comes.

Even though they only last for a few months, the pools provide homes and food for birds, turtles, otters, manatees (marine mammals), and fish, such as this wolf fish.

## Dune dwellings

A few hundred people live in small villages in the Lençóis Maranhenses. In the dry season, they raise goats and chickens, which wander through the sand. They also grow crops, such as cashews and cassava. In the rainy season, when farming is difficult, they head out to sea to go fishing.

The villagers live in huts built from mud, wood, and palm leaves collected from trees along the coast.

## Dune creatures

### Yellow armadillo

The yellow armadillo uses the powerful claws on its front feet to dig burrows and search for insect prey in the sand.

### White-eared opossum

Opossums are marsupials. They give birth to tiny babies that crawl into their mother's pouch to feed and develop.

### Maranhão slider

The Maranhão slider is a turtle. In the rainy season, it makes a long, risky journey from the forest to the lagoons to breed.

Meghalaya Root Bridges, India

# MEGHALAYA ROOT BRIDGES

In the forested hills of Meghalaya, northeast India, communities are linked by a series of extraordinary bridges constructed from the intertwined roots of living trees. The bridges are incredibly strong and long-lasting, and, in the monsoon season, they are the only way of crossing rivers and gorges.

The bridges are made from the roots of Indian rubber trees. These trees have roots underground and ropelike roots above ground that hold them like anchors.

Ropelike roots

# HOME OF THE CLOUDS

## Building bridges

To cross the rivers and link their isolated villages, the people here make bridges from the natural materials around them: the living roots of Indian rubber trees. Over many years, roots that are growing above ground are pulled, tied, and trained to grow a certain way, creating bridges, sturdy enough to take the weight of 50 people.

The name "Meghalaya" means "home of the clouds". This forest area is warm, humid, and, with an average of 12,000 mm (470 in) of rain each year, one of the wettest places on Earth. Heavy rain falls during the monsoon season, turning the paths into mud, and the rivers that criss-cross the hills into raging torrents.

The roots above the ground grow from trunks. They are pulled and tied by hand, and trained to form bridges that last for centuries.

## MORE BUILDING WITH TREES

### Jembatan Akar Bayang, West Sumatra, Indonesia

This bridge over the Batang Bayang River in Indonesia is made from the roots of two trees. They grow around a bamboo frame.

Khasi people make a naturally processed, high quality silk called Eri silk, using fibre from the cocoons of moths. The silk is woven on handlooms and used for traditional clothing.

## Sacred nature

The Khasi people, Jaintia people, and Garo people who live here have a close connection to their natural environment, and consider the forest to be sacred. This respect continues at home. In one village, Mawlynnong, household waste is collected in bamboo bins, then recycled as fertilizer for farmers' fields.

Rufous-necked hornbill

## Meghalaya wildlife

The hills and forests of Meghalaya are home to wild Asian elephants and the very rare clouded leopard. There are also deer, bears, gibbons, jackals, and monkeys. Among the reptiles that roam here are cobras, pythons, and monitor lizards, and there are hundreds of species of birds, including hornbills, vultures, and kingfishers.

Clouded leopard

Asian elephant

## Chapel Oak, Seine-Maritime, France

This ancient oak tree in France has hollow parts inside it in which there are two small chapels. They are reached via a spiral staircase around the tree trunk.

## Willow Palace, Auerstedt, Germany

To construct the Willow Palace in Germany, young willow trees were woven together and trained to form a dome. Training trees to grow a certain way is often used for building structures.

Wolfe Creek Crater, Australia

# WOLFE CREEK CRATER

On the edge of the Great Sandy Desert in Western Australia lies a giant crater. Scientists believe it was created when a massive meteorite crashed into Earth. This desert region has one of the harshest climates on Earth. Summer temperatures can reach a roasting 48°C (118°F). Groundwater in the middle of the crater allows trees and shrubs to grow there.

Scientists believe a meteorite hit Earth here, creating an almost circular crater with a rim around it.

# METEORITE STRIKE

Wolfe Creek Crater is as deep as a 20-storey building and measures around 875 m (2,800 ft) across. Scientists estimate that the meteorite that crashed here must have been about 15 m (50 ft) wide, weighed more than 50,000 tonnes (56,000 US tons), and travelled at around 15 km (10 miles) per second.

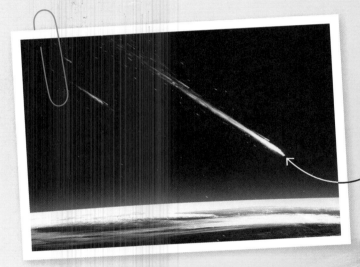

Scientists believe the meteorite crashed some 120,000 years ago.

Meteor

## Meteoroid, meteor, meteorite?

Sometimes chunks of rock or metal from space fall through the Earth's atmosphere. They are called meteoroids. Most burn up on the way, creating bright streaks of light called meteors. If a meteoroid reaches the ground, it is called a meteorite.

Meteorite

WOLFE
METEORITE

## MORE GREAT CRATERS

### Barringer Crater, USA

At around 1,200 m (4,000 ft) across, the Barringer Crater in Arizona, USA is the largest meteorite crater in the world.

## Dreamtime stories

The Djaru and Walmajarri people of the Great Sandy Desert are the traditional custodians (owners) of the land here. They have many Dreamtime stories about how the crater formed. One Dreamtime story tells how the crater was made when a giant snake slithered up through the Earth and raised its head above the ground.

## Crash landing

The force of the meteorite hitting the Earth triggered a huge explosion. It shattered rocks deep below ground and sent debris flying, some of which landed kilometres away. Scattered around the crater itself are rusty balls of rock containing iron thought to come from the meteorite.

# CREEK CRATER

Scarlet-chested parrot

Many birds and animals, such as dingoes and goannas (lizards), have adapted to desert life. The scarlet-chested parrot doesn't need to drink water. It gets moisture from the plants it eats.

## Vredefort Crater, South Africa

One of the world's oldest impact craters, Vredefort Crater in South Africa dates back more than 2 billion years.

## Tin Bider Crater, Algeria

Different layers of rock can be seen in the Tin Bider Crater, which sits in the Sahara Desert, Algeria. Geologists think Tin Bider is probably an impact crater.

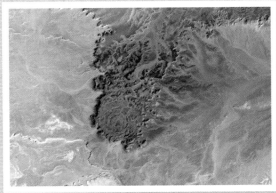

Mount Roraima, along the border of Brazil, Venezuela, and Guyana

# MOUNT RORAIMA

In northern South America stands a tabletop mountain that looks like an island floating above the clouds. Mount Roraima rises out of the rainforest. At its summit, there is a lost world of strangely shaped rocks and boulders, swamps, lakes, and unusual plants and animals.

On the summit of Mount Roraima, rocks have been weathered into fantastical shapes.

# TABLETOP

Mount Roraima is a tepui — a flat-topped mountain with sheer, steep sides. It stands 2,810 m (9,219 ft) tall, and its vast, flat summit is covered in huge black boulders and bare sandstone, with a few scattered bushes. In the tropical climate here, it rains almost every day. There are swamps, rivers, and lakes, and spectacular waterfalls that pour over the cliffs.

## Local lore

The white clouds and mist swirling around Mount Roraima give it a mysterious appearance. The people living in this region have many myths and legends about this extraordinary place. In some, it is the home of the mother goddess. In others, it is the stump of a giant tree that crashed to the ground, causing a terrible flood.

## How Mount Roraima formed

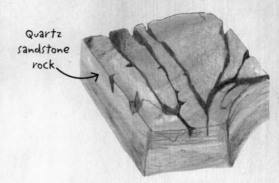

Quartz sandstone rock.

Over time, quartz sandstone in this area was broken down by rain, rivers, streams, and groundwater.

Mount Roraima

Rain, rivers, streams, and groundwater eroded weak sections of the rock, breaking the rock down through cracks.

After some 1.5 billion years, the erosion left behind flat, tabletop mountains, including Mount Roraima.

A waterfall cascading down the side of Mount Roraima.

Tepui means "house of the gods".

## Exploring caves

In 2003, a group of cavers exploring Mount Roraima made an extraordinary find. They discovered the entrance to one of the world's longest systems of quartz caves. The Cueva Ojos de Cristal (Cave of the Crystal Eyes) extends for almost 11 km (7 miles) inside the mountain.

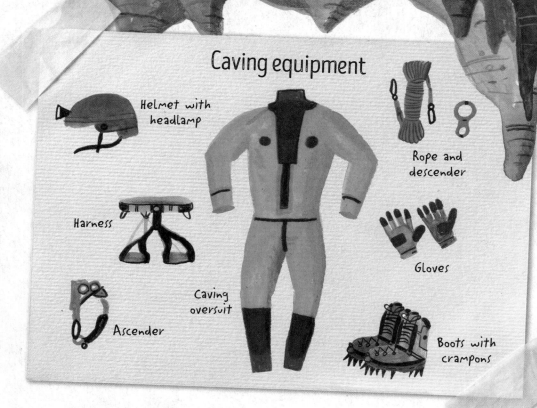

### Caving equipment

Helmet with headlamp

Rope and descender

Harness

Gloves

Ascender

Caving oversuit

Boots with crampons

Bladderwort
(Utricularia campbelliana)
growing on a tree

## Splendid isolation

Since its formation millions of years ago, Mount Roraima has been cut off from other areas due to its height. This has made it a unique habitat for plants and animals, including a beautiful type of carnivorous sundew – a plant that traps and digests insects, and the tiny Roraima bush toad. Usually seen on rocks, this toad is only found on the summit of Roraima and another nearby tepui.

Carnivorous sundew

South American pitcher plant

The Roraima bush toad curls into a ball and rolls away if threatened.

Ngorongoro
Crater, Tanzania

# NGORONGORO CRATER

Named after the Maasai word for the sound made by a cow bell — "ngoro ngoro" — this vast volcanic crater lies in the East African Rift Valley in Tanzania. The floor of the crater is now grassland, and is home to some of Africa's rarest and most iconic animals.

The crater is in the Ngorongoro Highlands, which are wetter and cooler than surrounding lower areas. The climate is subtropical (warm and wet with mild winters).

# VOLCANIC ACTION

The Ngorongoro Crater is the world's biggest caldera. Calderas are large craters that form after a volcano collapses. The Ngorongoro Crater is thought to have formed around 2.5 million years ago when a huge volcano erupted and collapsed in on itself. The crater covers an area of 264 sq km (102 sq miles).

## Life in the crater

The crater is home to an abundance of wildlife, including some of Africa's most famous animals, such as lions, elephants, zebra, and wildebeest. There are also around 30 critically endangered black rhinoceros, protected from poachers by armed guards. Animals thrive here because there is plenty of water from springs, streams, and rivers, which are fed by run-off from the crater's rim.

## How the crater formed

On the site of the crater, a volcano erupted violently.

The volcano started to crack as it erupted.

The volcano originally formed when lava from previous eruptions became solid.

As hot liquid lava rose up from the magma chamber, the chamber began to empty.

A small amount of magma remained.

A crater formed.

Solid lava

When the magma chamber emptied, the volcano was no longer supported by magma, causing the whole volcano to collapse and forming a crater.

Plants

Solid lava

Today, plants grow inside the large, bowl-shaped crater.

Some hot liquid lava remains beneath the crater.

Animals come to drink at the crater's waterholes.

Hippopotami

Flamingos

Black rhinoceros

118

A reconstructed skull belonging to an ancestor of humans, found in the Olduvai Gorge

Olduvai Gorge

## Olduvai Gorge

A short drive from the crater lies the Olduvai Gorge, one of the world's most important prehistoric sites. It was here, in the 1950s and 60s, that some of the earliest human remains were discovered, dating back millions of years. This led scientists to believe that the first human beings evolved in Africa.

## Maasai herders

The crater is a protected nature reserve, but the Maasai people, who have lived in the region for hundreds of years, have grazing rights there for their livestock. Cattle are very important in Maasai life and culture. The Maasai eat their meat and drink their milk. Cattle are also a sign of a person's wealth and status.

The Maasai move around, finding the best grazing spots. Their huts are easy to build and rebuild. They're made using branches covered in mud and cow dung, with grass for the roofs.

Wildebeest

Valley of the Geysers, Russia

# VALLEY OF THE GEYSERS

Jutting out into the sea in the far northeast of Russia is the Kamchatka Peninsula. This remote wilderness is famous for stunning volcanoes, lakes, and wildlife, and for the Valley of the Geysers — one of the largest groups of geysers and hot springs in the world.

Velikan (Giant), the biggest geyser in the valley

Geysers are hot springs that send steam and jets of hot water into the air. Learn about their formation on p.44.

# GUSHING GEYSERS

The Valley of the Geysers lies in the far east of the Kamchatka Peninsula among a chain of volcanoes. At 8 km (5 miles) long, it has around 90 geysers, as well as steaming mud pots and hot springs. The largest geyser, Velikan (Giant), blasts jets of water into the air that are up to 40 m (131 ft) high. (Find out more about geysers on pp. 43–45.)

Around 180 km (112 miles) from the Valley of the Geysers, Koryaksky is one of the volcanoes of Kamchatka. It towers over the city of Petropavlovsk-Kamchatsky.

## Volcanoes of Kamchatka

The Kamchatka Peninsula lies on the Ring of Fire around the Pacific Ocean. Here, one plate of the Earth's crust is sliding under another, causing volcanic eruptions and earthquakes. There are more than 300 volcanoes in this area, around 40 of which are still active. The highest is Klyuchevskoi, which erupts almost continuously.

Boiling pools of mud, called mud pots, are found throughout the valley.

## Rivers and lakes

Kamchatka has thousands of rivers and lakes, fed by rainfall and melting mountain snow. In summer, huge numbers of sockeye salmon lay eggs in the rivers and lakes. The salmon are a rich source of food for sea eagles and brown bears.

### Sockeye salmon

When laying their eggs, sockeye salmon change colour from silvery-blue to red and green.

### Kamchatka brown bear

Weighing up to a tonne, these bears use their paws to hook salmon out of rivers. They also feed on berries, as well as nuts from trees.

### Steller's sea eagle

This large eagle perches high. When it spies a fish, it dives down to catch it in its sharp talons.

## Natural disaster

Even though it can only be reached by helicopter, the Valley of the Geysers is a popular tourist attraction. But, in June 2007, disaster struck when a huge mudslide buried many of the geysers and springs. Luckily, Velikan was not affected, and parts of the valley are slowly recovering.

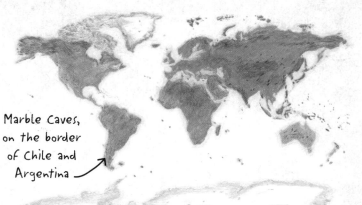

Marble Caves, on the border of Chile and Argentina

# MARBLE CAVES (CUEVAS DE MÁRMOL)

Carved out of marble rock, on the edge of Lake General Carrera, is a set of stunningly beautiful natural caves. Travel to this remote spot on the border of Chile and Argentina to experience the shimmering blue shades of rock. The three main caves are the Chapel, the Cave, and, the biggest of the three, the Cathedral.

Chapel cave

The Chapel cave and Cathedral cave are at the base of rocky islands. They get their names from their sculpted ceilings, church-like pillars, and ornate walls.

# MARBLE CARVING

The Marble Caves have been carved from marble rock by the constant lapping of the lake's waves. Over more than 6,000 years, water has seeped into cracks in the marble. These cracks have widened, eventually becoming large enough for waves to wash in, forming the caves.

The caves are carved into rocky islands at the lake's edge and into a peninsula that juts into the lake.

The different caves can only be reached by boat.

Cathedral cave

## MORE COOL CAVES TO EXPLORE

### Skaftafell ice cave, Iceland

This breathtaking ice cave is in a glacier. As the glacier moves along, so does the cave. It was carved when meltwater ran through and under the glacier. This process is still happening today.

The weather on the lake is slightly warmer than the cold, humid climate around it. But winds can blow up suddenly, and heavy clouds bring rain.

## Lake blues

Lake General Carrera covers an area of 1,850 square km (710 square miles). It is one of the largest lakes in South America. Fed by glaciers in the surrounding Andes Mountains, the water is cold, clear, and turquoise blue. The colour is caused by tiny particles of silt, ground out of rocks that the glacier passes. As the glacier ice melts, the particles are suspended in the water, and refract the blue part of sunlight hitting the lake.

## Cavernous colours

The walls of the Marble Caves are covered in swirls of blue. Amazingly, the marble is actually light grey. But it appears blue because of the reflection of the blue lake. The colours change through the year. They are brightest in summer (September to February), when the ice melts and the lake's water level rises.

People visit the caves in tourist boats. It's also possible to go by kayak. The water can be choppy, and it's best to set off in the morning when it's usually less windy.

## Eisriesenwelt ice cave, Austria

Inside Hochkogel Mountain in the Austrian Alps is the Eisriesenwelt, the world's largest ice cave. The first kilometre of the cave is a maze of passages, dripping with icicles.

## Mount Erebus ice caves, Antarctica

Mount Erebus is an active volcano in Antarctica. Steam from the volcano creates ice caves in its sides. They're close to the surface under a thin layer of ice.

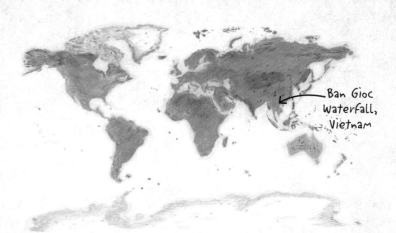

Ban Gioc Waterfall, Vietnam

# BAN GIOC WATERFALL

On the Quây Sơn River between China and Vietnam, Ban Gioc Waterfall plunges down a three-tiered cliff, amongst limestone peaks and lush valleys. After heavy rain, the falls reach full flow and thunder down the cliff side. The falls are in Non Nuoc Cao Bang Geopark, which has a hot, sticky tropical climate, with two seasons — dry and rainy.

Bamboo rafts take visitors close to the falls.

# FALLING WATER

With a drop of 30 m (100 ft), and around 300 m (985 ft) wide, Ban Gioc is Asia's biggest waterfall. It flows over a limestone cliff. Waterfalls form when rivers flow over rocks that erode at different speeds. The water erodes soft rock at the bottom more quickly, leaving a hard rock ledge above, over which the water plunges.

## Spirit world

Not far from Ban Gioc is Tongling Grand Canyon. Its name means "Connected to the Spirit World". You enter through a large cave, with a roaring underground river. In the past, the cave was used as a hide-out for local bandits.

The cave at Tongling Grand Canyon leads to a dense tropical rainforest and on into an enclosed world of gorges, cliffs, and waterfalls.

## How waterfalls form

River

Hard rock ledge

Soft rock

Broken rocks

Plunge pool

Over time, some of the hard rock ledge erodes and broken rocks fall into the plunge pool.

Water buffalo are used here to plough rice fields, ready for a new harvest.

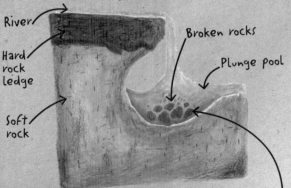

The Vietnamese mossy frog lives in this area. It clings to moss-covered rocks, looking like a clump of moss, hidden from predators.

## MORE FABULOUS FALLS

### Asik-Asik Falls, Philippines

Hidden by rainforest until 2010, the Asik-Asik Falls in the Philippines rush down a cliff covered in bright-green, water-loving plants.

Along the banks of the river, people live in small villages and farm the land. Rice is grown in fields on flat terraces, which are watered by the river.

## Winding river

The falls are fed by the beautiful, jade-blue Quây Sơn River, which winds for nearly 90 km (56 miles) along the border between China and Vietnam. On its way, it flows through spectacular mountains, green bamboo forests, and fertile rice fields.

## Dettifoss, Iceland

Dettifoss in Iceland is one of the most powerful waterfalls in Europe. Fed by meltwater from a nearby glacier, it crashes 44 m (144 ft) into a steep-sided canyon.

## Murchison (Kabalega) Falls, Uganda

At Murchison Falls in Uganda, the Victoria Nile River bursts through a narrow gap in the rocks before tumbling into a deep pool. The river then flows into Lake Albert.

Socotra Archipelago, Yemen

# SOCOTRA ARCHIPELAGO

In the Indian Ocean, 350 km (220 miles) from Yemen's coast, lies the Socotra Archipelago, with a habitat like nowhere else on Earth and some of the rarest plants and animals in the world. An archipelago is a place containing a group of islands. In the Socotra Archipelago, there are four islands. The largest by far is called Socotra.

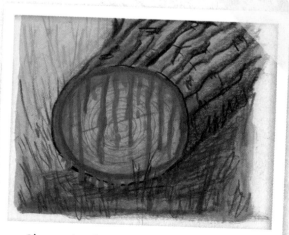

Bizarre-looking dragon's blood trees dot the islands of the Socotra Archipelago. They get their dramatic name from their bright red sap.

# ISLANDS APART

The islands that make up the Socotra Archipelago were once part of the prehistoric supercontinent of Gondwana. They broke away around 20 million years ago, and the wildlife evolved in isolation. This is why today many plants and animals on the islands are found nowhere else. The harsh climate is classed as desert, and is hot, dry, and windy. On the island of Socotra, the landscape includes coastal plains, a limestone plateau, and jagged mountains.

Around 90% of the Socotra Archipelago's reptiles, including the Socotra chameleon, are only found on the islands.

The unique wildlife found on the islands makes the Socotra Archipelago one of the most precious centres for biodiversity on the planet.

On Socotra Island, land snails climb trees to escape from the heat and predators such as beetles.

The Socotra sunbird is unique to the archipelago. It has small yellow tufts near its shoulders.

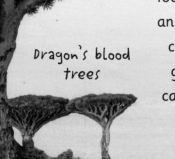

Dragon's blood trees

## Fragile future

Today, the Socotra Archipelago and its wildlife face an uncertain future. The islands are threatened by civil war in Yemen, introduced animals (such as goats), and climate change. Powerful cyclones cause flooding and destroy fragile coral reefs and island plants, including dragon's blood trees.

## Hoq Cave art

For thousands of years, the island of Socotra was an important stop on trade routes between India, the Middle East, and Africa. In 2001, a team of scientists from Belgium made an amazing discovery. In Hoq Cave, a large cave on the island, they found hundreds of short inscriptions scratched on the rocks by sailors and traders.

Inside Hoq Cave, sailors carved their names on the rocks. There are also a few drawings of ships.

## Here be dragons

A third of the plants on the Socotra Archipelago only grow on the islands, among them the famous dragon's blood tree. Able to live for a thousand years, it looks like a strange alien plant growing on the rocky slopes.

Dragon's blood tree

Upturned branches hold the tree's leaves high, so that they can collect moisture from the rolling mists.

Boswellia tree

Bottle tree

Smoking Hills, Canada

# SMOKING HILLS

Along a stretch of Arctic coast in remote northwest Canada, thick plumes of smoke rise from striking, red-striped cliffs. The rocks here have been smouldering away for hundreds, if not thousands, of years. But what is causing them to burn?

Although known as the Smoking Hills, the hills are actually cliffs. Their red stripes are created by iron-rich minerals in the rocks.

# BURNING ROCKS

In the 1850s, Arctic explorer Robert McClure spotted the Smoking Hills from his ship while searching for survivors of an earlier expedition. Hoping the smoke came from cooking fires, he sent a landing party to check. They found no signs of life, but brought some of the smouldering rocks back to the ship, one of which burned a hole in McClure's wooden desk.

The Smoking Hills are difficult to get to. Today, there are still no roads to the area. It can only be reached by helicopter, seaplane, or boat.

## So what makes the rocks burn?

At first, scientists thought volcanic activity was making the cliffs burn. Later, they discovered that the cliffs are formed from shale rocks, rich in sulphur and coal. Over time, these rocks are worn away by the weather. This exposes them to oxygen in the air and causes the sulphur and coal to spontaneously catch fire.

For years, Inuvialuit people who live near the hills have been collecting the rocks for fuel. Their nearest settlement (above) is called Paulatuk, which means "place of coal".

## Acid conditions

In the surrounding Arctic tundra, there is much wildlife, but very little survives on the slopes of the Smoking Hills. Large amounts of sulphur dioxide are released when the rocks burn, making any soil and rain here highly acidic. Only a few species of plants have adapted to the tough conditions, including wideleaf polargrass and stinkweed.

Wideleaf polargrass is able to grow in the acidic soil.

Stinkweed leaves can neutralize (make less acid) any acid rain that falls on them.

## Polar pingos

Pingos are small, cone-shaped hills on the Arctic tundra. They form where frozen ground is forced upwards by water in the ground beneath it. Pingos grow very slowly and can take hundreds of years to reach 60 m (200 ft), their maximum height. They can last for 1,000 years before they finally break down and collapse.

A pingo collapses when its core of ice melts, leaving a ring of tundra around a small lake.

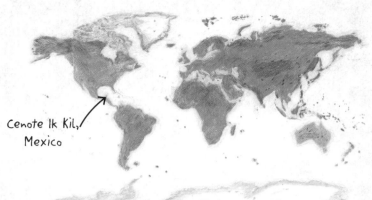

Cenote Ik Kil, Mexico

# CENOTE IK KIL

Cenote Ik Kil lies on the Yucatan Peninsula in Mexico. Perfect for swimming, it's a large natural pool with sheer rock walls, open to the sky and surrounded by a curtain of vines and waterfalls. "Cenote" is a Mayan word that loosely translates to "sinkhole". Thousands of cenotes dot the Yucatan Peninsula. They vary in size and shape.

During the time of the Mayan Empire, a cenote was a place of sacrifice to Chaac, the Mayan rain god.

# SINKING FEELING

Cenotes (natural sinkholes) form when surface limestone rock collapses, exposing underground rivers. The water is very clear as it comes from rainwater that has filtered through the ground. Some cenotes are open to the sky. Others are entered through small holes in the ground.

Cenote Ik Kil is about 60 m (200 ft) across.

## How cenotes form

Cenotes form when soft limestone rock near the surface of the land collapses.

Rainwater feeds into the rivers through cracks and gaps in the rock.

This is due to underground rivers eroding and carrying away the soft limestone underneath.

During high tide, the sea also enters the limestone through cracks, causing the rock to break and collapse at an even faster rate.

## Sacred cenotes

Cenote Ik Kil is close to the ancient Mayan city of Chichen Itza. In the Mayan language, "ik kil" means "place of the winds". For the Maya, cenotes were not only major sources of water, but also sacred entrances to the underworld. Human bones and jewellery have been discovered in Ik Kil — all offerings to the rain god, Chaac.

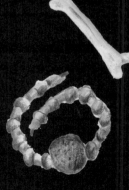

Human sacrifices were an important part of Mayan rituals.

From the top of Cenote Ik Kil it is about 26 m (85 ft) down to the water.

## Spectacular habitat

The Yucatan has a hot tropical climate, with a dry season and a humid wet season. Breezes blow along the coast. The rainforests here are home to many birds and monkeys, while the cool cenote water is great for catfish and frogs.

Motmot

Beautiful birds, such as toucans, parrots, and motmots, live around the cenote.

You can swim with the catfish at Cenote Ik Kil and dive down to explore a spectacular underwater world. Stalactites and stalagmites line the caverns.

## Cave of the Jaguar God

In 2019, at nearby Chichen Itza, archaeologists made an astonishing discovery under the Mayan ruins. They uncovered a secret network of caves known as Balamku, or "Jaguar God", and, after hours spent crawling through the tight tunnels, they found a treasure trove of more than 150 objects used in Mayan rituals some 1,000 years ago.

Over the years, stalagmites have grown around some of the objects. Learn more about stalagmites and stalactites on pp.60—61.

Some Mayan objects found at Balamku caves

143

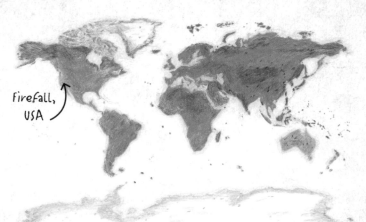

Firefall, USA

# FIREFALL

Every February, if conditions are right, Horsetail Falls in Yosemite National Park, California, USA, appears to transform into a flaming fall of fire. This famous waterfall can only be seen like this briefly at sunset, glowing like liquid fire as it flows down the side of El Capitan, a massive block of granite rock.

Like many of the waterfalls in Yosemite, Horsetail Falls only flows for part of the year (winter and early spring) because it is fed by melting snow.

Horsetail Falls

El Capitan

El Capitan, the site of the Horsetail Falls, is one of the high granite rocks in Yosemite. It stands around 900 m (3,000 ft) tall. It was carved by glaciers around 1 million years ago. Some parts of it are slowly breaking away.

# MAJESTIC YOSEMITE

Horsetail Falls is one of hundreds of waterfalls in Yosemite. The park covers almost 3,100 square km (1,200 square miles) of California's Sierra Nevada mountains. As well as its waterfalls, it's known for its giant trees, deep valleys, and high granite rocks. The climate is Mediterranean, with warm, dry summers, and wet, snowy winters.

You can hike or climb to the top of the granite rock El Capitan. Amazing rock climber Alex Honnold climbed it without ropes or safety gear!

Mule deer

The light from the setting sun hits the waterfall.

## Horse tail of liquid fire

For a few days in February, Horsetail Falls is transformed. At sunset, the sun's rays reflect off the water to create a stunning orange "firefall". This only lasts for about 10 minutes, and conditions must be just right, with clear skies and plenty of melted snow to feed the waterfall.

### Waterfall to Firefall

The setting sun's light hits the falls, and the water reflects the orange light (the arrow shows the direction of the sunlight). The sun is only at the right angle to do this for a few days in February.

## Ribbon Falls

On the other side of El Capitan is Ribbon Falls, said to be the longest single-drop fall in the USA. It plunges 491 m (1,612 ft) down the rock face in spring. Fed by melting snow, it can dry up in the summer.

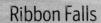

Sequoia trees

Bobcat

Yosemite is famous for its giant sequoia trees, some of which may be more than 3,000 years old. It is also home to more than 400 species of animals.

Skeleton Coast,
Namibia

# SKELETON COAST

The Skeleton Coast in Namibia spans more
than 500 km (300 miles). It is spectacular,
but treacherous. Over the years, it has
become a graveyard for countless animals
and ships. The coast got its name from
the whale and seal bones that lie here,
once common finds when these animals
were hunted, but the name also aptly
describes the ghostly shipwrecks.

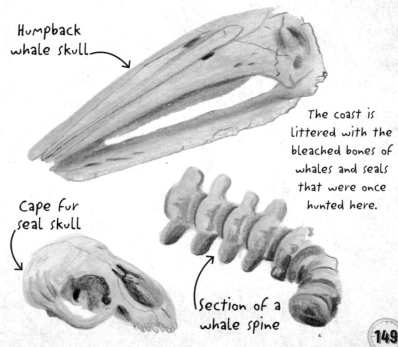

Humpback
whale skull

The coast is
littered with the
bleached bones of
whales and seals
that were once
hunted here.

Cape fur
seal skull

Section of a
whale spine

149

# DESERT MEETS SEA

The Skeleton Coast in Namibia lies between the Atlantic Ocean and the sand dunes of the Namib Desert. Here, huge waves crash onto the shore, strong winds blow, and thick fog rolls in off the sea. Cold water, from a cold ocean current, cools the hot desert air, causing the fog to form. In this windy, desert climate, little rain falls, but the fog provides a precious supply of freshwater.

Towering sand dunes meet the sea along the Skeleton Coast, and fog rolls in, covering the desert.

## How the fog forms

Hot desert air is cooled by the cold water.

A cold ocean current, called the Benguela Current, cools the hot desert air.

Skeleton Coast

Cold Benguela Current

Fog forms and rolls in over the Skeleton Coast.

All air contains water vapour, and when the desert air cools, the vapour changes to tiny drops of liquid, creating the fog.

Shipwreck

Whale vertebrae

## Bones and wrecks

As well as the whale and seal bones on the Skeleton Coast's shore, the thick fog, stormy seas, and unpredictable currents have led hundreds of ships to their doom here. Some wrecks are buried, some have rotted away, but other haunting relics remain, ranging from 15th century Portuguese wooden boats to modern steel fishing ships and cargo ships.

## Unexpected wildlife

Despite the tough conditions, many animals live along the coast, including lions (which hunt kudu as well as seals here), hyenas, and jackals, and elephants that sometimes wade in the waves. There are also plants, such as lithops, that depend on the fog for moisture.

Hyena

Kudu (a species of antelope)

Lithops

Lithops, or "pebble plants", are brilliantly camouflaged to avoid being eaten.

Cape fur seal

African elephant

Jackal

The sea here is rich in plankton and fish, vital for this habitat's food chain. The fish are eaten by Cape fur seals at Walvis Bay (at one end of the Skeleton Coast).

Shipwreck (MV Dunedin Star)

The wreck of the UK cargo ship MV Dunedin Star hit the ground of the Skeleton Coast in 1942 and got stuck there.

The shipwrecks remain because it is difficult to clear them away. But more recent wrecks are being removed to help keep the coast clean and safe.

Chinoike Jigoku, Japan

# CHINOIKE JIGOKU

Chinoike Jigoku is one of a cluster of steaming hot springs in the city of Beppu, Japan. Its name means "Blood Pond Hell", from its bright-red, boiling-hot water. The pond is far too hot to bathe in. The water reaches temperatures of around 78°C (172°F) – twice as hot as a warm bath. But it is a truly spectacular sight.

The vivid red colour of the spring water is caused by iron oxide in the ground.

# CITY OF SPRINGS

The Japanese word for hot spring is "onsen". There are thousands of onsen all over Japan because the country lies on the Ring of Fire along the Pacific Ocean and has many active volcanoes. In the city of Beppu alone, there are around 3,000 onsen, gushing out more than 130,000 tonnes (143,300 US tons) of hot water every day. Find out more about hot springs on pp. 47–49 and pp. 161–163, and learn more about the Ring of Fire on p. 122.

While Chinoike Jigoku is unsuitable for bathing, you can bathe in other onsen. Water in the safe springs has health benefits for the skin. Onsen mud is also thought to be good for the skin.

## Hellish ponds

Eight of the hot springs in Beppu are known as "jigoku" (hells) because of their appearance. Apart from Chinoike Jigoku, another of the most dazzling is Umi Jigoku (Sea Hell). The very bright blue colour of this spring comes from a substance called iron sulphate (a type of salt that is made from iron) in the water.

Sea Hell

## Keeping warm

In Jigokudani Monkey Park, Japanese macaques regularly bathe in hot springs where the water is safe for them to go in. For a long time, scientists believed this helped them keep warm in the bitterly cold winter. They now think that it also helps the monkeys to lower their stress levels.

Japanese macaques, also called snow monkeys, have thick fur and can survive temperatures as low as -20°C (-4°F).

Manjanggul Cave, South Korea

# MANJANGGUL CAVE

Almost 2 million years ago, a massive volcanic eruption created the island of Jeju in South Korea. Today, evidence of this explosive event can be seen across the island. Apart from its main volcano, Jeju has around 360 smaller cones and more than 160 lava tubes, including the Manjanggul Cave, the longest lava tube in Asia.

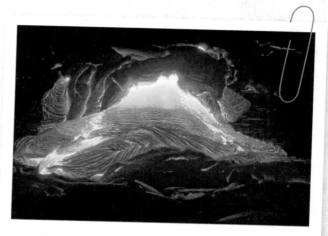

Today, at places in the world where volcanoes are active, hot liquid lava flows through hardened lava and creates tunnels, in the same way as on Jeju 2 million years ago.

# LAVA FEATURES

The Manjanggul Cave snakes underground for more than 13 km (8 miles). Its walls and ceiling are rounded, as if they have been scooped out. Inside are different features, created when the hot liquid lava became solid, including stalactites, stalagmites, and a pillar almost 8 m (25 ft) tall.

A tall pillar formed when hot lava dripped through a hole in the tube ceiling and then became solid. More lava then dripped down and solidified, building up into a pillar.

Lava flowing into a hole in a lower level of the tube hardened to create a lava rock formation known as the elephant's foot.

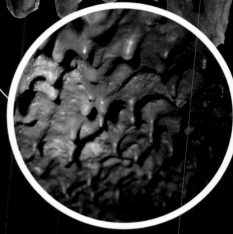

Stalactites are rock formations that hang from cave ceilings. They don't just form in lava caves. See pp.60—61 for stalactites created by rainwater in another type of cave.

Common bent-wing bats can hunt in the dark. They rest in the cave's ceiling.

Stalactites formed when the tube's lava ceiling melted due to the heat of more hot lava flowing into the tube. The melted ceiling then hardened into stalactites.

## Cave creatures

Some animals are perfectly suited to the damp, cold, dark conditions inside Manjanggul Cave, including around 30,000 common bent-wing bats. They find their way in the dark using echolocation — they work out the position of things by how long it takes for noises they make to bounce off objects and come back as echoes. Nutrients in their droppings support other animals, such as the recently-discovered Jeju cave spider.

## How a lava tube forms

A lava tube is a tunnel, created by slow-moving, liquid lava flowing through hardened surface lava. At the end of a volcanic eruption, the lava supply stops. Any remaining lava drains away, leaving a tube-like cave behind.

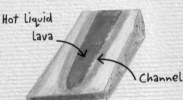

Hot liquid lava

Channel

1. Liquid lava flows from a volcanic eruption and creates channels of lava in the ground like the one above.

Hot liquid lava

2. More hot lava flows and stacks on top of existing hot lava, creating layers and making the channel bigger.

Solid lava at the top and sides

Hot liquid lava

Tube shape

3. Lava at the top and sides cools and hardens. More hot lava flows and builds up, melting into the ground. This creates a tube shape.

Solid lava crust

4. More lava at the top and sides cools, eventually forming a crust over the tube at the surface.

Hollow, tube-like cave

5. The eruption ends. The lava stops flowing and drains away, leaving a hollow tube.

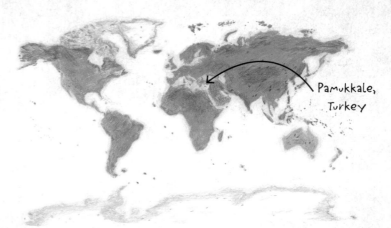

Pamukkale,
Turkey

# PAMUKKALE

Pamukkale in southwest Turkey is a spectacular natural landscape in the Menderes River valley. "Pamukkale" means "cotton castle" in Turkish, and it's easy to see how this magical place got its name. A series of shimmering white terraces, topped with warm, turquoise pools, cascades down the steep slope of the river valley.

The terraces are created by limestone deposits that build up over time. The limestone is in spring water that flows down the valley side.

# TRAVERTINE TERRACES

The white terraces at Pamukkale are made of a particular type of limestone called travertine. This forms when hot, mineral-rich spring water rises to the surface, then flows down the Pamukkale slopes, depositing calcium carbonate. The calcium carbonate crystallizes into travertine. (See pp. 47–49 and pp.153–155 for more hot springs.)

Travertine forms at hot springs, but it can also form near streams, waterfalls, and at cold springs.

As the travertine builds up, in places it looks like solid, white waterfalls.

## MORE TRAVERTINE TERRACES

### Huanglong, China

Along the Huanglong Valley in Sichuan, China, travertine terraces wind their way between snow-capped mountains and thick forests.

## How a travertine terrace forms

Hot water forms a pool.

Water from the pool cascades down the slope.

The calcium carbonate in the water crystallizes into travertine.

Over time, the travertine creates step-like terraces.

Older springs can become blocked off.

Hot spring water (containing calcium carbonate) rises.

Dazzling white travertine

## Pamukkale pools

The Pamukkale terraces start at nearly 200 m (660 ft) high on the valley side and run down to the lower valley. There are numerous terraced pools formed from 17 hot springs, and the temperature of the water ranges from a warm 35°C (95°F) to a roasting 100°C (212°F).

## Thermal waters

Since ancient times, the hot spring water at Pamukkale has been valued for its healing properties. Just above the terraces lie the ruins of the Greek-Roman city of Hierapolis and the Antique Pool where Cleopatra may have bathed more than 3,000 years ago. Today, most of the natural pools are off limits for bathing, to prevent damage by the large number of visitors.

In the Antique Pool where bathing is allowed, you can swim over ancient columns that were sent crashing down by an earthquake long ago.

The climate at Pamukkale is Mediterranean with hot, dry summers and mild winters, perfect for swimming where bathing is allowed.

## Mammoth Hot Springs, USA

The travertine terraces at the Mammoth Hot Springs in Yellowstone National Park, USA, were formed over thousands of years.

## Badab-e Surt, Iran

The travertine terraces at Badab-e Surt in Mazandaran, Iran, are rust-coloured because of deposits of iron in one of the springs that created them.

163

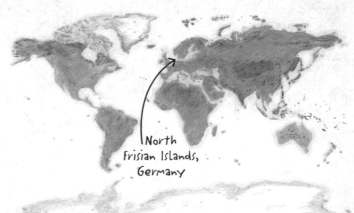

North Frisian Islands, Germany

# NORTH FRISIAN ISLANDS

In the Wadden Sea, off the north coast of Germany, is a group of storm-battered islands called the North Frisian Islands. For centuries, people have lived here, fishing and farming. Today, tourists come to see the thatched villages, sand dunes, and mudflats, as well as the many seabirds and seals on the islands.

When the tide goes out here, vast areas of mud are revealed around the grass-covered islands.

# SHIFTING ISLANDS

The North Frisian Islands are an archipelago – a place made up of a group of islands. There are four larger islands – Sylt, Föhr, Amrum, and Pellworm – and ten islets (tiny islands). The islands are the remains of mainland or former, larger islands, eroded by waves and storms over hundreds of years. They continue to change shape today. The islands have an oceanic climate, with mild summers and cool winters.

## Magical mudflats

Twice a day, the tide goes out, exposing vast stretches of mud called mudflats, also known as tidal flats. During low tide, you can walk across the mud from island to island. These are some of the world's largest mudflats. When the tide comes in, they flood with seawater again. The plants and animals that live here have had to adapt to the constantly changing conditions.

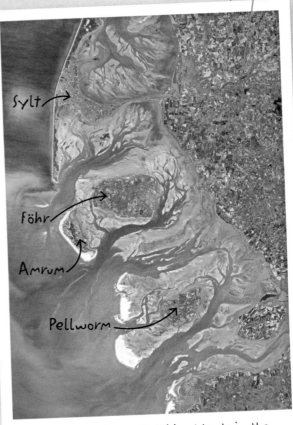

Sylt

Föhr

Amrum

Pellworm

The four main North Frisian Islands in the Wadden Sea are Sylt, Föhr, Amrum, and Pellworm. A causeway connects Sylt to the mainland.

## Under threat

Like many islands around the world, the North Frisian Islands are under threat from climate change. With storm surges and rising sea levels washing away huge amounts of sand along the coasts, they could eventually disappear. In many places, coastal defences, including dams and pumps, have been installed to help prevent flooding.

## Island wildlife

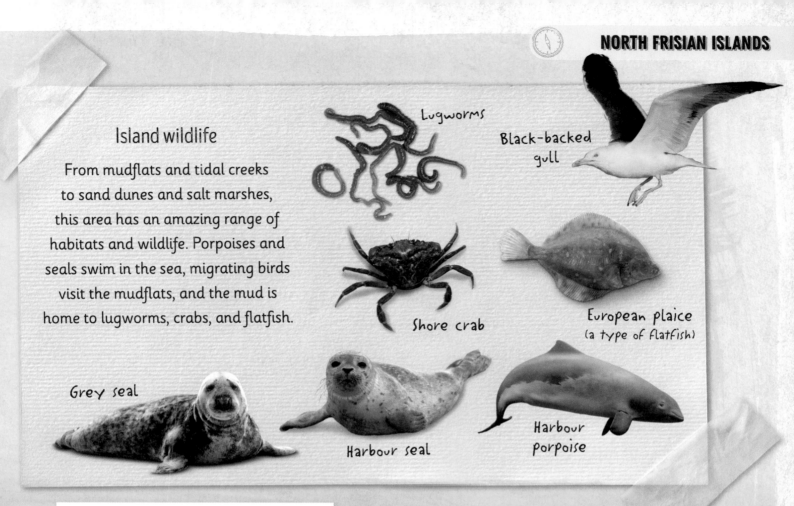

From mudflats and tidal creeks to sand dunes and salt marshes, this area has an amazing range of habitats and wildlife. Porpoises and seals swim in the sea, migrating birds visit the mudflats, and the mud is home to lugworms, crabs, and flatfish.

Lugworms

Black-backed gull

Shore crab

European plaice (a type of flatfish)

Grey seal

Harbour seal

Harbour porpoise

As waves go out to sea, they pull sand and stones with them.

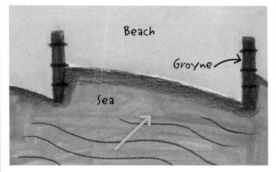

Beach

Groyne

Sea

The sand and stones are then pushed further along the shore by the waves coming back in. Groynes help to stop the sand and stones from moving along the beach.

The waves push the sand and stones in the direction shown by the blue arrow.

## Longshore drift

The shape of the islands' coastlines is always changing because of longshore drift. This is when ocean currents push sand and stones along a beach. The material is first picked up from the beach by the backwash (the waves going out to sea), and then it's carried back by the swash (the waves coming in) to form new beach further on.

In this view of Pellworm Island, you can see the groynes—the low walls that act as coastal defences and stop longshore drift eroding the shore.

# GLOSSARY

## algae
Various plants and organisms (living things), which grow in or near water; some types of algae can only be seen under a microscope, others grow up to 50 m (164 ft).

## archipelago
Large group or chain of islands; the islands are usually small.

## arid
Another word for dry; a place that gets very little or no rain.

## atmosphere
Layer of gases surrounding the Earth that reach a height of around 1,000 km (620 miles).

## bacteria
Microscopic (tiny), single-celled organisms (living things) that live in soil, water, or on plants or animals.

## basalt
Type of dark, fine-grained rock that forms when lava from volcanoes becomes solid.

## biodiversity
Variety of plant and animal life in a particular place or in the world.

## calcium carbonate
White powder found as the mineral, calcite; it is found in rocks such as limestone, chalk, and marble.

## cassava
South American plant with thick roots that is grown for food and used to make flour.

## cavern
Large, deep cave formed by underground water; or a large chamber in a cave.

## clay pan
Naturally forming layer of clay just below the surface of the ground that holds water after heavy rain.

## climate change
Changes in Earth's climate, especially a rise in temperature caused by high levels of carbon dioxide and other gases in the atmosphere.

## continental crust
Parts of the Earth's crust that lie under the continents.

## coral reef
Rocky ridge built by tiny animals, called coral polyps, in shallow, tropical seas.

## crater
Large bowl-shaped hole at the top of a volcano; or a large bowl-shaped hole created when a big object hits the ground.

## crystal
Solid, natural material that forms into a geometrical (regular patterned) shape; crystals can form in rocks.

## desert
Region, often covered with sand or rocks, where very little rain falls and few plants can grow.

## drought
Long period of time during which a place gets little or no rain.

## erode
When wind, ice, or moving water (or a combination of these things) erode, they wear away rocks and soil; any moving water can erode rocks and soil – rain, the sea, rivers, or lakes.

## erosion
Process by which rocks and soil are worn away by wind, ice, or moving water (or a combination of these things); any moving water can erode rocks and soil – rain, the sea, rivers, or lakes.

## evaporate
When a liquid evaporates, it is heated and changes into a gas.

## flash floods
Sudden, fast-flowing floods caused by unusually heavy rain.

## geology
Study of the rocks that make up the Earth, their physical structure and history; geologists study geology.

## geometric
Word describing a pattern or shape made up of regular shapes or lines, such as a chequered pattern, a square, or a cube.

## geopark
Landscape of outstanding geological interest, together with the community that live there; areas with geopark status have a plan of action to help local people understand and promote their area and care for its environment.

## geothermal
Word describing something connected to the heat that comes from inside the Earth.

## glacier
Large, moving mass of ice on land formed from a build up of firmly packed snow on mountainsides or near the poles; glaciers move slowly downhill, often down mountains, due to the influence of gravity and their own weight.

## glacier meltwater
Water flowing from the melted ice of a glacier.

## gneiss
Type of rock that contains layers of minerals, such as quartz.

## Gondwana
Supercontinent that existed from around 550 to 180 million years ago.

## gorge
Deep valley, with steep sides, formed by flowing water, such as a river, or by rain breaking down rocks.

## granite
Type of very hard, grey, pink, or black rock, made mostly of quartz.

## groundwater
Water found underground in soil, rock, or sand.

## ice age
Time in the past when the climate became very cold and ice covered large parts of the Earth; there have been several ice ages.

## ice sheet
Enormous glacier, the size of an entire continent, that covers everything with ice.

## ice shelf
Large area of ice floating on the sea, attached to land ice (glaciers or an ice sheet); ice shelves are fed by glaciers or an ice sheet.

## impermeable

Word describing a substance that does not allow gases or liquids to pass through it.

## irrigation

Process of bringing water to fields and farmland so that plants and crops can grow.

## jade

Green precious stone from which jewellery and ornaments can be carved.

## lagoon

Area of sheltered seawater, almost cut off from the sea by coral, rocks, or sand.

## lava

Hot, liquid rock from inside the Earth that reaches the surface due to volcanic activity.

## limestone

Type of white or light grey rock, often used as a building material.

## magma

Hot, liquid rock deep inside the Earth; it can rise to nearer the surface.

## methane

Gas with no colour or smell; one of the gases contributing to climate change and global warming (the rise in Earth's temperature caused by gases in the atmosphere).

## microscopic

Word describing something so small that it can only be seen under a microscope.

## mineral

Solid chemical substance formed in the ground; most rocks are made of minerals.

## monsoon

Season when monsoon winds carry heavy rain to countries in southern Asia.

## oceanic crust

Parts of the Earth's crust that lie under the oceans; thinner than continental crust.

## peninsula

Long piece of land that sticks out from the mainland into a sea or lake.

## phytoplankton

Tiny plants that float near the surface of the sea, rivers, or lakes; many sea creatures feed on phytoplankton.

## pigment

Substance that gives a particular colour to something.

## plateau

Large area of flat land that stands out above the surrounding landscape.

## prehistoric

Word describing a period in history that was a very long time ago and before people wrote things down.

## quartz

Hard, clear mineral.

## quartz sandstone

Sandstone rock that is mostly made of quartz.

## rainforest

Forest that grows in a tropical region and gets a large amount of rain.

## reflect

When a surface reflects, it sends light back, rather than absorbing the light.

## rift valley

Valley that is formed by movement of the Earth's crust; rift valleys have steep sides.

## run-off

Water that flows across the surface of the land rather than being absorbed by the ground.

## salt pan

Naturally forming, flat area of ground that is covered with salt.

## sandstone

Type of rock made mostly of particles of sand.

## sea level

Height of the surface of the sea.

## sinkhole

Hole in the ground where rock or soil has been worn away by water.

## subtropical

Word describing places on Earth that lie to the north and south of tropical regions; subtropical places are often warm and have a wet season.

## supercontinent

Huge, single landmass made up of all the land on Earth in prehistoric times.

## tectonic plates

Gigantic pieces of the Earth's crust.

## temperate

Word describing places on Earth that are between the poles and the tropical regions; these places have a wider temperature range and distinct seasonal changes compared to other regions on Earth.

## tropical

Word describing regions on Earth on either side of the equator; the tropics normally have a very small yearly temperature range and usually only two seasons – a wet and a dry season.

## wavelength

Distance between the crests (high points) of waves; light and sound have wavelengths.

## weathering

Physical or chemical breakdown of rocks; causes of weathering include changes in temperature, rain, ice, and plants.

# INDEX

# ACKNOWLEDGEMENTS

**DK would like to thank:** Caroline Twomey for proofreading and Helen Peters for the index.

The publisher would like to thank the following for their kind permission to reproduce their photographs:

(Key: a=above; b=below/bottom; c=centre; f=far; l=left; r=right; t=top)

**123RF.com:** 143702428 161br, andreykuzmin 25tr (map), San Hoyano 127cr, Konstantin Kalishko 134-135b, lorcel 147tl, picsfive 17 (note), 21b (note), 29 (Note), 36-37 (Note), 41t, 57cb (Note), 60-61b (Note), 65tr (Note), 68c (Note), 73r (Note), 76-77b (Note), 82c (Note), 83tr (Note), 86b (Note), 94r (Note), 103b (Note), 106-107b (Note), 110-111b (Note), 115t (Note), 123 (Note), 130-131b (Note), 139t (Note), 142cla (Note), 151t (Note), 155t (Note), 162-163b (Note), 167t (Note), seamartini 98ca, spumador71 36bl, thais1986 29tl;
**Alamy Stock Photo:** 146crb, Agefotostock / Iñaki Caperochipi 90l, Agefotostock / John Higdon 22-23, All Canada Photos / Jason Pineau 139b, Alpineguide 140-141, blickwinkel / Baesemann 136-137, Danita Delimont, Agent / Claudia Adams 150bc, Ulrich Doering 53tl, 116-117, dpa picture alliance 143br, Philip Game 68bl, Thomas Garcia 38-39, 41, Global Vibes 32crb, Harley Goldman 86-87, Martin Harvey 57crb, Image Professionals GmbH / Per-Andre Hoffmann 14-15, Image Source / Yevgen Timashov 80-81, Imagebroker / Arco Images / TUNS 91cla, imageBROKER / Holger Weitzel 164-165, imageBROKER / Martin Siepmann 126br, imageBROKER / Peter Giovannini 94bc, INTERFOTO / Personalities 25tr, Inge Johnsson 42-43, JohnWray 37tr, Andrey Khrobostov 19br, Christophe Kiciak 106br, Chris Mattison 115bc, mauritius images GmbH / Nico Stengert 107bc, mauritius images GmbH / Pölzer Wolfgang 13c, Hazel McAllister 91ca, Minden Pictures 50-51, 86cb, 112-113, Juan Carlos Muñoz 53c, Eric Nathan 32cb, Natural History Collection 86clb, Nature Picture Library / Alex Mustard 10-11, 12-13, Nature Picture Library / Alex Mustard / 2020VISION 37clb, Nature Picture Library / Chadden Hunter 127bc, Nature Picture Library / Doug Perrine 30-31, Nature Picture Library / Michel Roggo 24-25t, Nature Picture Library / Solvin Zankl 61cla, George Ostertag 45cr, Paul Mayall Australia 108-109, Christian Pauschert 166tr, Peter O'Donovan 91tl, Prisma by Dukas Presseagentur GmbH / Heeb Christian 41tc, Reuters / Mohamed Abd El Ghany 67br, Juergen Ritterbach 118-119, Robertharding / Michael Runkel 158clb, Russotwins 109br, Sabena Jane Blackbird 119tl (skull), Scott Sady / Tahoelight.com 43br, Science History Images / Photo Researchers 139crb, Science Photo Library / Ton_Aquatic, Choksawatdikorn 48cr, Top Photo Corporation 81tr, Travel Pix 62-63, Travelart 31br, Universal Images Group North America LLC / Planet Observer 110br, 111bc, Yoshiko Wootten 152-153, Xinhua / Zhao Dingzhe 66-67, Solvin Zankl 167cr; **Depositphotos Inc:** luiza.lisnic.gmail.com 111tr, shalamov 56cr; **Dorling Kindersley:** Bill Peterman 73cla, Ruth Jenkinson and Peter Anderson and 123RF.com: stevanzz 151ca; **Dreamstime.com:** Anakondasp 29ftl, Vorasate Ariyarattnahirun 126bl, Chris De Blank 55br, Bukki88 39br, Jeremy Campbell 162br, Charm Moment 28-29, Ckchiu 105br, Daboost (All spreads- Background), Davemhuntphotography 130cb, 167ca, Nadiia Diachenko 17tr, Digitalpress 130c, Eastmanphoto 69bl, Elena Ray Microstock Library © Elena Ray 86bc, Hdanne 167cl, Hpbfotos 47crb, Idreamphotos 64br, Isselee 37cb, 151c, Vladislav Jirousek 57clb, Jelena Jovanovic 95clb, Dmitrii Kashporov 115crb, Tanya Keisha 29crb, James Kelley 60br, Anna Komissarenko 77bc, Iuliia Kuzenkova 82-83, Leonovdmn 76bl, Lunamarina 145br, M K 68-69, Mady Macdonald 138crb, Robyn Mackenzie / Robynmac 12cla (Tape), 13c (Tape), 20 (Tape), 29 (Tape), 33tc (Tape), 36clb (Tape), 40cra (Tape), 41 (Tape), 57tr (Tape), 60clb (Tape), 72tr (Tape), 73tc (Tape), 76clb (Tape), 80tr (Tape), 81c (Tape), 87tr (Tape), 94tr (Tape), 95cl (Tape), 98clb (Tape), 103 (Tape), 106 (Tape), 110clb (Tape), 111tr (Tape), 119tc (Tape), 122cl (Tape), 123crb (Tape), 126clb

(Tape), 127cr (Tape), 130 (Tape), 133crb (Tape), 138crb (Tape), 143 (Tape), 150cla (Tape), 155tc (Tape), 159 (Tape), 162clb (Tape), Hugo Maes 16crb, Aliaksandr Mazurkevich 104-105, Mikelane45 167tr, Aitor Muñoz Muñoz 34-35, Perseomedusa 151cra, Veronika Peskova 17ca, Plotnikov 16cb, Rabor74 150tr, Dmitry Rukhlenko 73cr, Martin Schneiter 40, Elena Skalovskaia 103tr, Stephen Smith 40cr, Aleksey Suvorov 82clb, Tampaci 11br, Thejipen 158, Tihayanadya 81clb, Tiplyashina 80clb, Aleksandar Todorovic 95tl, Anastasiia Tymashova 142-143c, Jorn Vangoidtsenhoven 87bc, Olga N. Vasik 121br, Wirestock 68crb, Belinda Wu 72-73, Yobro10 151cl, Krisma Yusafet 153br; **FLPA:** Fabio Pupin 134tr; **Don Funk (Alpine Climber):** 76br; **Getty Images:** 500Px Plus / Maddy M. 46-47, AFP / Vasily Suvorov 120-121, AFP / Wang Zhao 73crb, Barcroft Media / Riau Images 106bl, Barcroft Media / Victor Lyagushk 60bl, Bettmann 65clb, EyeEm / Mark Fitzpatrick 74-75, Chung Sung-Jun 159tl, Moment / nespyxel 33tr, Moment / RBB 106-107, Moment / Sergio Pessolano 92-93, Anton Petrus 78-79, Photodisc / PhotoStock-Israel 28clb, Stone / Angelo Cavalli 148-149, Universal Images Group / Auscape 76tr; **Getty Images / iStock:** 3quarks 165br, 167br, 4045 130-131, 4kodiak 146-147, AndreAnita 82cb, aphotostory 70-71, Astalor 56-57, Bibhash Banerjee 13cl, Bborriss 123tr, Artur Bogacki 69crb, Worawat Dechatiwong 73tr, DennyThurstonPhotography 45cla, Dgwildlife 82crb, E+ / brittak 119cra, E+ / raisbeckfoto 117br, E+ / tanukiphoto 154tr, Mario Faubert 52-53, Forplayday 110cla, glebchik 82cl, gorsh13 69br, Emma Grimberg 29fcl, HomoCosmicos 36br, Jana_Janina 21tr, Janos 49tr, Jason_YU 99crb, JeremyRichards 126-127, Katharina13 75br, kavram 56tl, 87tr, James Kelley 41cb, kenhophotographer 128-129, LaserLens 130bl, leonardospencer 101br, LeoPatrizi 37cl, lindsay_imagery 76cl, LordRunar 16-17b, lu-pics 167c, mammuth 37tc, MarcelStrelow 58-59, Pedro Moraes 113br, nevskyphoto 98bl, oscity 110bl, peterkocherga 82ca, Prill 119tl, Ondrej Prosicky 57br, 143tr, Natalie Ruffing 37bc, Sanga Park 99br, SeanPavonePhoto 154, shalamov 155, ShantiHesse 94-95, Smitt 18-19, 20-21t, Gustavo Muñoz Soriano 35crb, Stanson 114, starush 162, Nicolas Tolstoï 137br, TopPhotoImages 162bl, ugurhan 163cr, VisualCommunications 106cl, VladKyselov 97br, vvvita

26-27, 29cl, 29fcla, Dennis Wegewijs 131bc, Panida Wijitpanya 102cr, Wojciech-P 143cra, zanskar 132-133; **naturepl.com:** Mark Moffett 134cr; **Keith Partridge:** 6cla; **Lightsparq Photography / Vijay Manohar:** 144-145; **Julian Jansen van Rensburg:** 135tl; **Science Photo Library:** Wim Van Egmond 32cra, Ted Kinsman 45c; **Shahrogersphotography.com:** Anup Shah 53clb; **Shutterstock.com**: akedesign 98-99, Andrey Armyagov 33cb, AzmanMD 156-157, Colin Bourne 76crb, Matteo Chinellato 110cb, chrisontour84 150-151, Yevhenii Chulovskyi 130br, ddg57 71br, Jakob Fischer 163bc, FJAH 158tr, 159tr, Niks Freimanis 61bc, Gregorioa 107tl, Guaxinim 127tl, Claude Huot 150c, Shaun Jeffers 49clb, JekLi 2-3, Iurii Kazakov 122clb, Ralf Lehmann 157br, Lukas Bischoff Photograph 44bl, McDow Photo Inc 147cb, Mirigrina 84-85, Ingrid Pakats 122-123, Suzanne Pratt 48bl, Luciano Santandreu 29cla, SAPhotog 57tr, Serjio74 124-125, Lauren Squire 102-103, Suksamran1985 160-161, TAW4 72tr, Pakawat Thongcharoen 100-101, TOMO 155tr, Nguyen Quang Ngoc Tonkin 96-97, 131tc, Jessica Towns 48-49, Juergen Wackenhut 166-167b, Oleg Znamenskiy 54-55; **SuperStock:** Minden Pictures 88-89; **U.S. Geological Survey / Bethany L. Burton:** 25clb

**Cover images:** *Front:* **Getty Images / iStock:** ixpert cl (globe); *Front and Back:* **Alamy Stock Photo:** Inge Johnsson bc; **Dreamstime.com:** Wirestock cr; **Getty Images / iStock:** Mario Faubert cl, MarcelStrelow ca, PavelSinitcyn bl; **Shutterstock.com:** Bruno Biancardi fcrb, Guitar photographer tr, Andrea Izzotti tl, lindamka br, PawelG Photo fbr, Nicola Pulham cla, Ricardo Reitmeyer cb, Dmitriy Rybin c, Scapigliata crb, Marcel Strelow tc; *Spine:* **Shutterstock.com:** Andrea Izzotti t, lindamka cb, PawelG Photo b, Nicola Pulham ca

All other images © Dorling Kindersley
For further information see:
www.dkimages.com

## About the author

Anita Ganeri is an award-winning author of children's information books. Her best-selling series, *Horrible Geography* (Scholastic Children's Books), won the Blue Peter Best Book with Facts in 2009. She is a Fellow of the Royal Geographical Society and the Royal Scottish Geographical Society. In 2010, she was awarded the Tivy Education Medal by the Royal Scottish Geographical Society for her "outstanding contribution to geographical education".

## About the illustrator

Tim Smart loves the natural world and has been drawing nature from a young age. His favourite drawings in this book are the whales. He does not have a favourite colour, but dark indigo and sandy yellow are always his most stumpy looking pencils. Tim has a big scruffy beard and lives in London with his two best friends, Katherine and Enid.